WHAT'S DIFFERENT

Find and circle **6** things that are diff

Picture A

Picture B

© School Zone Publishing 06339

CROSSWORD

Use the clues to fill in the puzzle.

Across

2. Which animal gives us wool?
5. Which animal has feathers?
6. Which animal likes to chase mice?

Down

1. Which animal do we ride?
3. Which animal likes to roll in mud?
4. Which animal has horns?

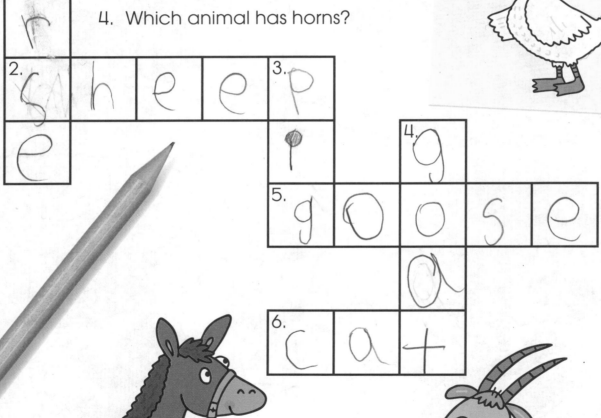

Crossword answers (handwritten):

1 Down: horse
2 Across: sheep
3 Down: pig
4 Down: goat
5 Across: goose
6 Across: cat

MAZE

Draw a line from start to finish.

FINISH

START

HIDDEN PICTURE

Find and circle the hidden pictures.

carrot   baseball bat   balloon   pizza   moon

star   candy   remote control   pencil   ruler

WORD SCRAMBLE

How many words can you make from the letters in ROAD TRIP ?

1. TOAD
2. RIP
3. DIP
4. ROAR
5. LIP
6. LIT

7. PO
8. DRIP
9. DOT
10. ROT
11. PIT
12. RAT

5 = GOOD   8 = GREAT   12 = BRILLIANT!

DOT-TO-DOT

Connect the dots from 1-25.
Color the picture.

PUZZLE IT OUT

Which shirt did the baseball team pick?

They do not like stripes.
They do not like the color red.
They don't want stars.
Purple is their favorite color.

MAZE

Draw a line from start to finish.

START

FINISH

SOLVE THE CODE

Use the code to solve the riddle.

CODE

	1	2	3	4	5
★	S	T	U	O	L
⬭	W	B	X	K	B
△	N	U	E	D	K
○	L	Z	P	G	D
▢	A	R	Y	I	C

What animal never needs a haircut?

 1   2   1   1   4 3 1 4 5 3

A __ A __ __ __ A __ __ __ __

WORD SEARCH

Look at the word list.
Circle the words in the puzzle.

WORD LIST

FRIEND	DAD
MOM	UNCLE
BROTHER	BABY
AUNT	SISTER

```
F X R D F R I E N D
R M D A D P S N Z O
Z G R N K Q E T H L
Y Z S U J K Z L A D
T C I N Z I C P U Z
K M S C L T X M N N
Q K T L B A B O T K
T W E E E I N M Z B
D B R O T H E R V G
B A B Y F Z B R N P
```

© School Zone Publishing 06339

WHAT DO YOU KNOW?

Read each sentence.
Circle **true** or **false**.

1. There are 4 robots in the picture.
   true   **false**

2. The blue robot has 3 arms.
   true   **false**

3. The green robot has yellow eyes.
   true   **false**

4. The red robot is the biggest.
   true   **false**

5. There is a purple robot.
   true   **false**

6. All of the robots have 2 arms and legs.
   true   **false**

WHAT'S DIFFERENT?

Find and circle **6** things that are different in **picture A** and **picture B**.

Picture A

Picture B

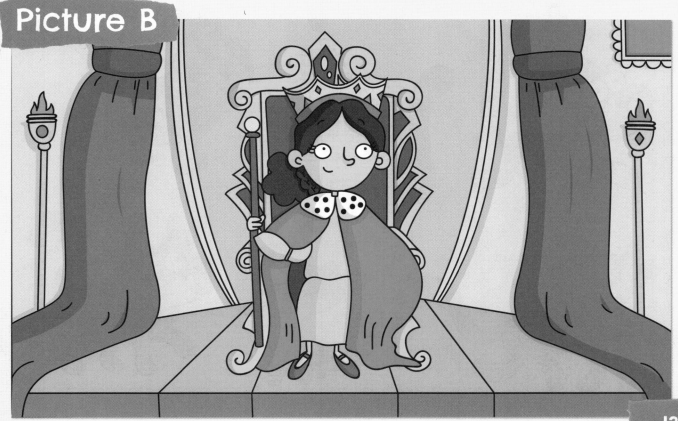

© School Zone Publishing 06339

MATCHING

Find and circle the
picture that looks
exactly like this one:

LEARN TO DRAW

Follow the sample picture in the grid to draw the picture below.
Color the picture.

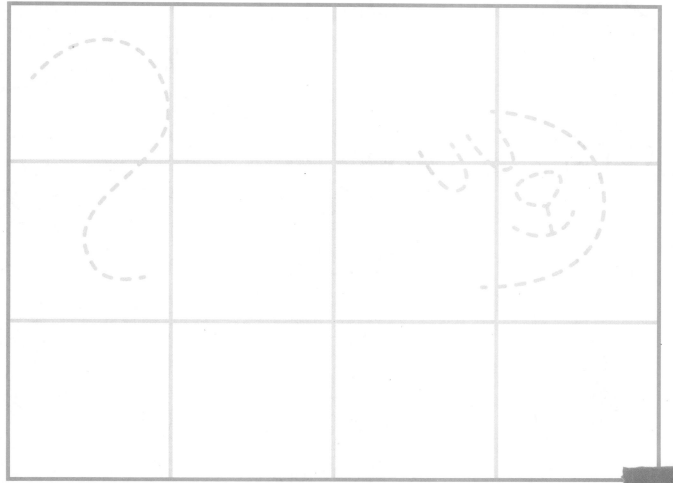

SEARCH

Look at the picture and write how many of each you can find.

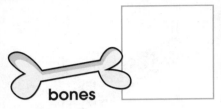
bones

butterflies

flowers

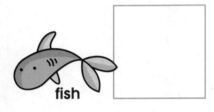
fish

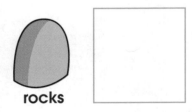
rocks

trees

16

SOLVE THE CODE

Follow the directions.
Then read the message that is left.

Color the **B** boxes red.
Color the **Q** boxes blue.
Color the **K** boxes green.
Color the **Z** boxes yellow.

K	H	O	W	Z	B	M	A	N	Y
Q	Z	M	O	N	T	H	S	K	B
A	R	E	Z	Q	B	K	I	N	Q
Q	B	A	K	Z	Y	E	A	R	?

Write the hidden message. Then answer the question.

_____

_____

DRAWING PUZZLE

Copy the drawing from each puzzle piece
to its matching place in the grid below.
Trace the dotted lines.
Color the picture.

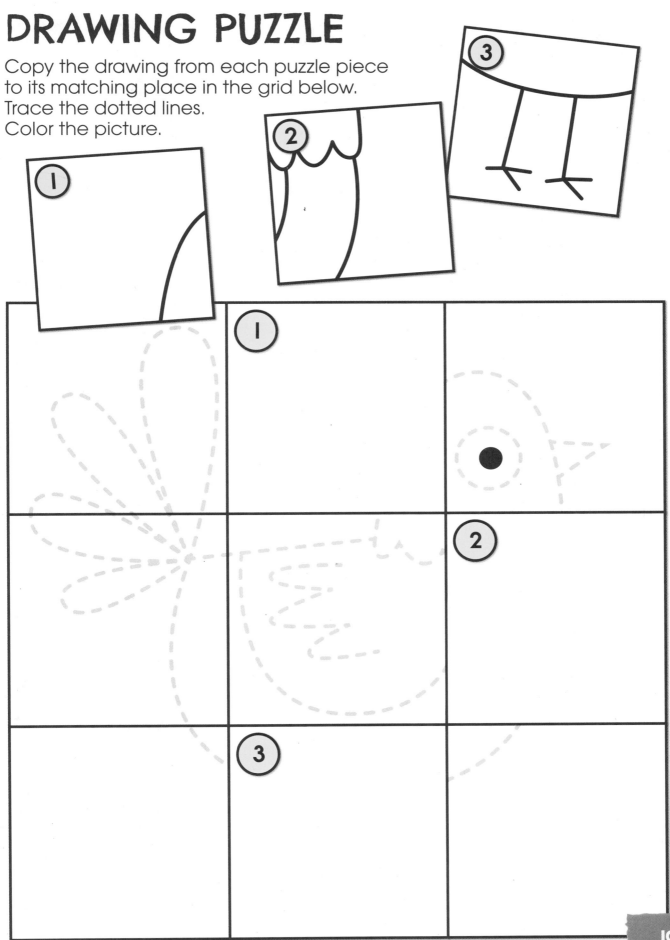

COLORING

Color the picture.

- ● = red
- ● = blue
- ● = green
- ● = orange
- ● = purple
- ● = black

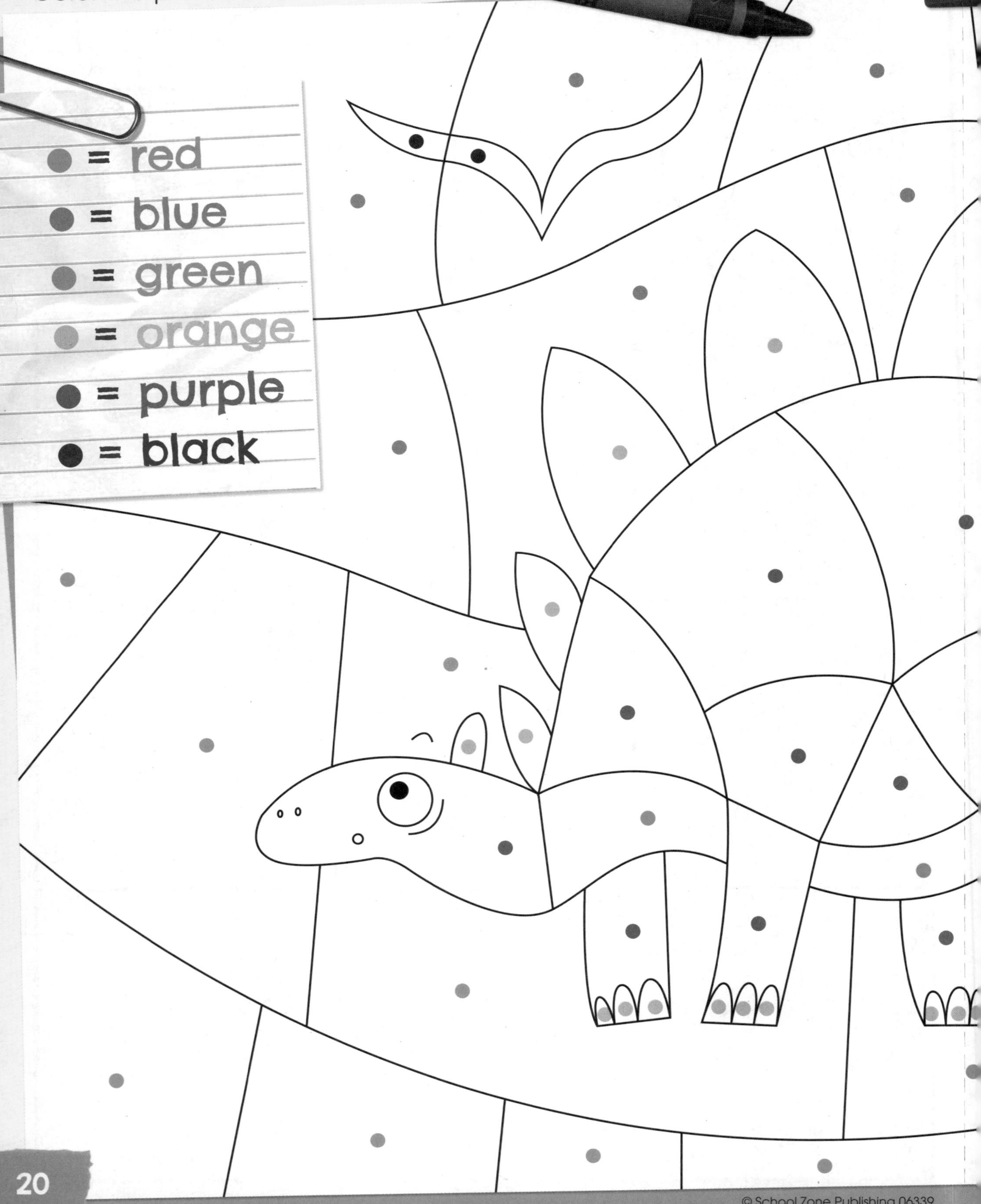

WHAT'S DIFFERENT?

Find and circle **6** things that are different in **picture A** and **picture B**.

Picture A

Picture B

WORD SEARCH

Look at the word list.
Circle the words in the puzzle.

```
L H E J L W U L S H
U W G V H Z J Q H C
Y N G H J Q H M O L
K P K R Z N O S E O
B L T I B A L L A W
D A C O R B Q K O N
H A T Z P D C H S L
I S B Y V U R I N G
F L O W E R P W J J
N G K C F U N B J W
N X V Z W P J E F Q
```

SOLVE THE CODE

Use the code to solve the riddle.

Code

	1	2	3	4	5
☆	O	W	B	U	I
●	N	J	G	T	Y
▲	H	W	O	L	C
●	Z	D	P	V	M
■	S	Z	F	K	F

Which are the most valuable fish?

3 ●   1 ☆   4 ▲   2 ●   5 ■   5 ☆   1 ■   1 ▲

___ ___ ___ ___ ___ ___ ___ ___

MATCHING

Find and circle the picture that looks exactly like this one:

MAZE

Draw a line from start to finish.

START

FINISH

WHAT'S DIFFERENT?

Find and circle **6** things that are different in **picture A** and **picture B**.

Picture A

Picture B

CROSSWORD

Use the clues to fill in the puzzle.

Across
1. What color rhymes with "true"?
3. What color is made with yellow and red?
4. What color rhymes with "seen"?

Down
1. What color rhymes with "clown"?
2. What color rhymes with "hello"?
5. What color rhymes with "bed"?

WORD LIST
blue   green   brown
orange   yellow   red

LEARN TO DRAW

Follow the steps to draw a frog.
Color the picture.

STEP 1:   STEP 2:   STEP 3:   STEP 4:   STEP 5:

MAZE

Draw a line from start to finish.

START

ROAD CLOSED

FINISH

WHAT'S DIFFERENT?

Find and circle **6** things that are different in **picture A** and **picture B**.

Picture A

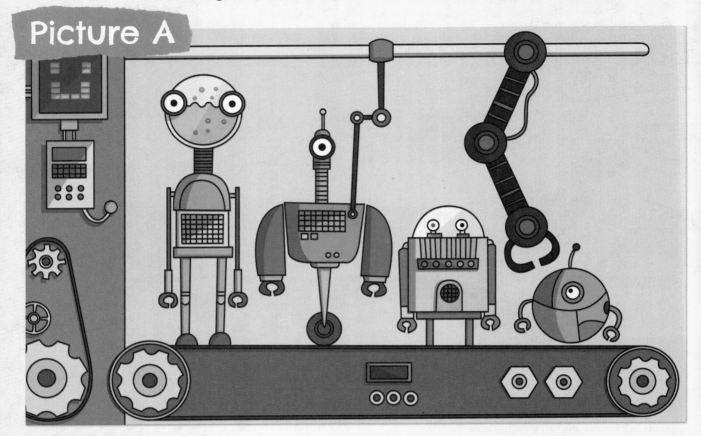

Picture B

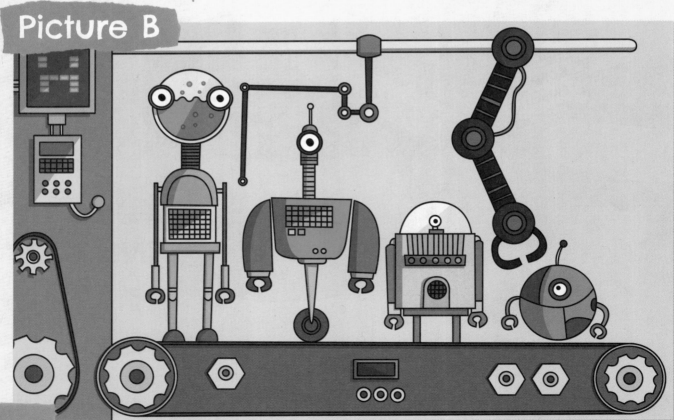

SOLVE THE CODE

Use the code to solve the riddle.

CODE

	1	2	3	4	5
★	W	L	X	R	E
⬭	I	A	P	H	Q
△	M	N	L	V	K
○	E	D	Y	Z	P
▢	C	L	D	B	H

What do you call an insect born in May?

2 ⬭   1 △   2 ⬭   3 ○   4 ▢   5 ★   5 ★

A ___ ___ ___ ___ ___ ___

PATTERNS

Circle the car to finish each pattern.

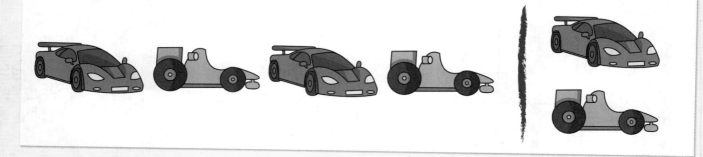

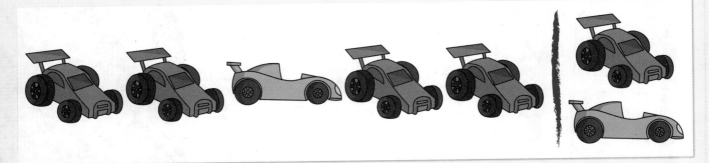

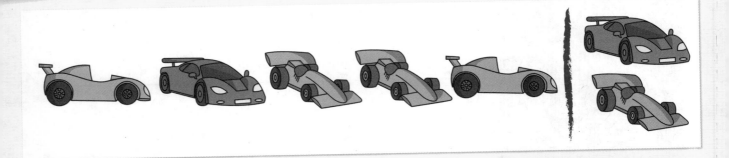

MAZE

Draw a line from start to finish.

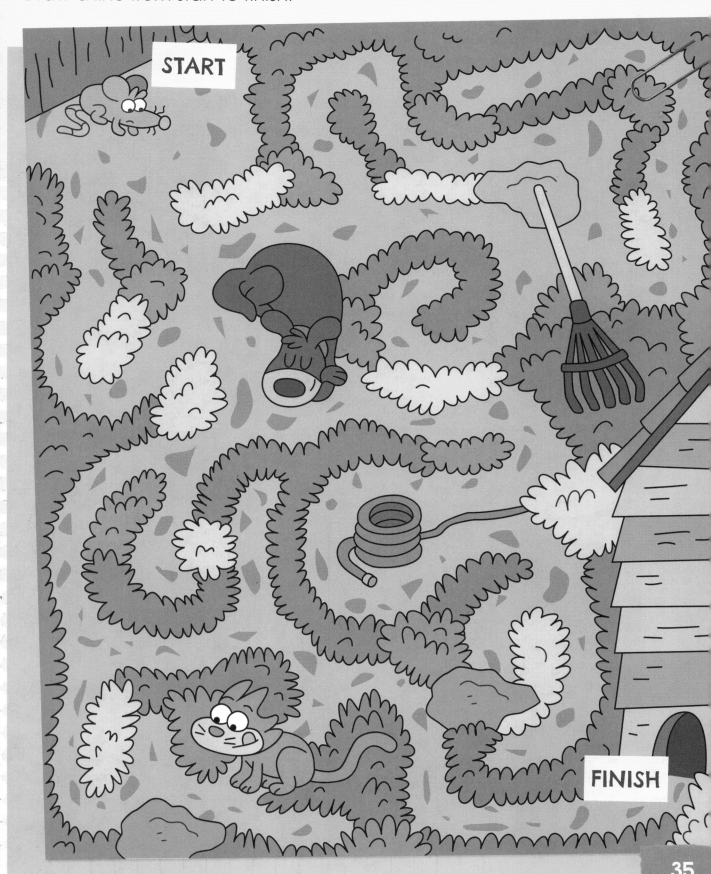

START

FINISH

HODGEPODGE

Each  has one that looks exactly like it.
Draw a line between each of the matching pairs.

Look at the picture on the left.
Color the graph for each one you find in the picture.

	1	2	3	4	5	6	7	8	9	10
🐸										
🌹										
🦋										
🐞										

Use the graph above to solve the problems.

🐸 + 🦋 = _____   🐞 + 🦋 = _____

🌹 + 🐞 = _____   🐸 + 🌹 = _____

 +  = _____

CROSSWORD

Use the clues to fill in the puzzle.

Across
3. I like to run in a wheel.
5. I am "man's best friend."
6. I run after mice.

Down
1. I like to swim.
2. I have feathers.
4. I have a hard shell.

40

WHAT'S DIFFERENT?

Find and circle **6** things that are different in **picture A** and **picture B**.

Picture A

Picture B

WORD SEARCH

Look at the word list.
Circle the words in the puzzle.

WORD LIST
BLACK
WHITE
BLUE
GREEN
YELLOW
RED
PURPLE
BROWN

L	G	Y	E	L	L	O	W	D
B	A	M	K	Y	H	T	H	G
G	N	B	L	A	C	K	I	H
R	C	U	R	Z	I	N	T	E
E	Q	F	B	L	U	E	E	O
E	I	C	S	Q	V	J	B	P
N	K	P	U	R	P	L	E	L
R	J	X	T	D	E	M	V	W
B	R	O	W	N	H	R	E	D

42

SOLVE THE CODE

Look at the pictures.
Write the names of the pictures in their numbered rows in the puzzle.
Use the code to solve the riddle. An example is done for you.

5. **fish**　　3. **crab**　　1. **whale**　　4. **turtle**　　2. **shrimp**

	A	B	C	D	E	F
5	F	I	S	H		
4						
3						
2						
1						

Which fish has five arms?

D　B　E　A　A　C　C　A　D　C　B
4　2　1　2　4　3　2　5　2　5　1

___ ___ ___ ___ ___ ___ ___ ___ ___ ___ ___

PATTERNS

Circle the picture to complete the patterns.

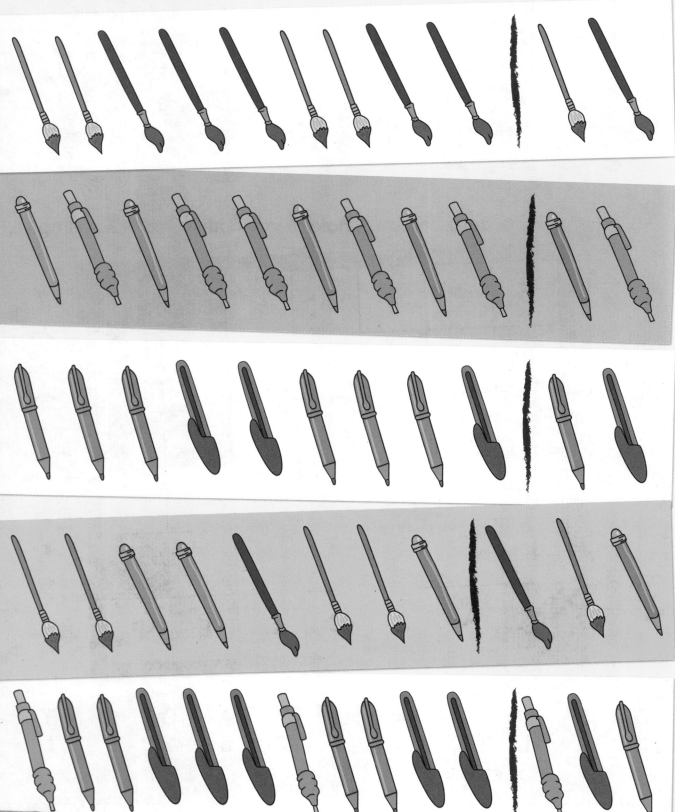

DOT-TO-DOT

Connect the dots from 1-30.
Color the picture.

HODGEPODGE

Each 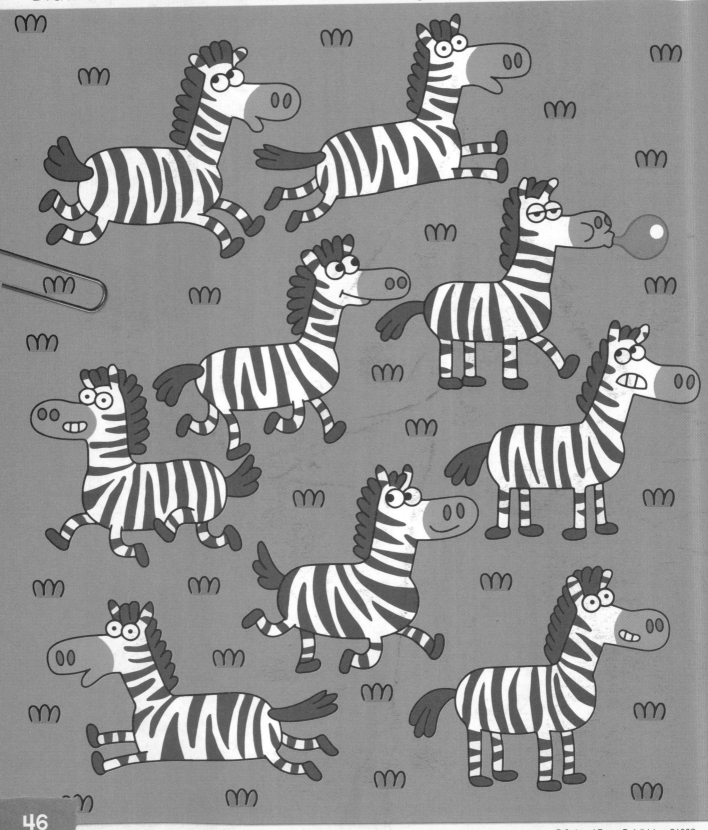 has one that looks exactly like it.
Draw a line between each of the matching pairs.

WHAT'S DIFFERENT?

Find and circle **6** things that are different in **picture A** and **picture B**.

Picture A

Picture B

SOLVE THE CODE

Look at the pictures.
Write the names of the pictures in their numbered rows in the puzzle.
Use the code to solve the riddle.

2. **bird**

3. **snail**

5						
4						
3						
2						
1						
	A	B	C	D	E	F

1. **rabbit**

5. **frog**

4. **bee**

What do you call a snail on a ship?

B	A	B	B	E	E	B	C
1	3	3	1	1	3	4	2

___ ___ ___ ___ ___ ___ ___ ___

WORD SEARCH

Look at the word list.
Circle the words in the puzzle.

```
L X X W K D R Y I H
P G X H H B H Y X C
G R A S S K P D M N
H B F Z F I R S S S
C R E A M T E H K B
I S H A K E Y F Y V
C J I N Z J M J J X
E U W A L K O N Q S
A S U M M E R M Z U
L U N O G V F A F N
I C E C R E A M W G
```

WHAT DO YOU KNOW?

Read each sentence.
Circle **true** or **false**.

1. 2 of the parrots are red.

   true   **false**

2. The blue parrot is the biggest.

   true   **false**

3. The red parrot is on the green parrot.

   true   **false**

4. All of the parrots beaks are yellow.

   true   **false**

5. The blue parrot has yellow on its tail.

   true   **false**

6. Both green parrots are flying away.

   true   **false**

WORD SEARCH

Look at the word list.
Circle the words in the puzzle.

WORD LIST
- BEE
- BEAR
- DEER
- FOX
- OWL
- RABBIT
- BAT
- DUCK

X	S	T	B	L	T	P	N	S	P
T	B	E	E	O	N	K	U	H	F
M	Q	O	A	M	F	G	X	M	O
I	O	V	R	S	T	D	U	R	X
X	W	C	L	B	P	G	R	Q	B
R	L	Q	R	A	B	B	I	T	H
B	A	T	Z	Z	O	D	K	L	B
O	H	J	G	D	U	C	K	O	N
U	X	T	F	G	Z	H	B	V	V
D	E	E	R	C	P	B	E	Q	F

MATCHING

Find and circle the picture that looks exactly like this one:

HIDDEN PICTURE

Find and circle the hidden pictures.

life ring   football   spatula   flashlight   hot sauce

backpack   tennis ball   sausage   banana   pizza slice

WORD SCRAMBLE

How many words can you make from the letters in CAMPING ?

1. _____

2. _____

3. _____

4. _____

5. _____

6. _____

7. _____

8. _____

9. _____

10. _____

11. _____

12. _____

5 = GOOD   8 = GREAT   12 = BRILLIANT!

LEARN TO DRAW

Follow the sample picture in the grid on the right to draw the picture below. Color the picture.

WHAT'S DIFFERENT?

Find and circle **6** things that are different in **picture A** and **picture B**.

Picture A

Picture B

WHAT DO YOU KNOW?

Read each sentence.
Circle **true** or **false**.

1. The giraffe has a long neck.
   true   **false**

2. The giraffe has spots.
   true   **false**

3. The giraffe has two legs.
   true   **false**

4. The giraffe has wings and can fly.
   true   **false**

5. The giraffe has a tail.
   true   **false**

6. The giraffe has three eyes.
   true   **false**

SOLVE THE CODE

Use the code to solve the riddle.

☆	U	E	B	R	Q	M
⬭	R	U	G	I	H	J
△	J	X	F	L	N	R
⬤	E	V	S	C	A	D
▢	K	T	Z	O	P	E
	1	2	3	4	5	6

Which animal drops from the sky?

5 ⬤   6 △   5 ⬤   4 ⬭   5 △   6 ⬤   2 ☆   6 ▢   1 ⬭

___ ___ ___ ___ ___   -   ___ ___ ___ ___

MATCHING

Find and circle the picture that looks exactly like this one:

WHAT'S DIFFERENT?

Find and circle **6** things that are different in **picture A** and **picture B**.

Picture A

Picture B

LEARN TO DRAW

Follow the steps to draw a rocket.
Color the picture.

STEP 1:

STEP 2:

STEP 3:

STEP 4:

STEP 5:

STEP 6:

WHAT'S DIFFERENT?

Find and circle **6** things that are different in **picture A** and **picture B**.

Picture A

Picture B

64

WHAT DO YOU KNOW?

Read each sentence.
Circle **true** or **false**.

1. Little Red Riding Hood is running through the forest.

   true   **false**

2. Little Red Riding Hood is running from a mouse.

   true   **false**

3. Little Red Riding Hood is wearing a blue hood.

   true   **false**

4. Little Red Riding Hood is riding a bicycle.

   true   **false**

5. The wolf is hiding behind a car.

   true   **false**

LITTLE RED RIDING HOOD

HODGEPODGE

Each  has one that looks exactly like it.
Draw a line between each of the matching pairs.

WHAT'S DIFFERENT?

Find and circle **6** things that are different in **picture A** and **picture B**.

Picture A

Picture B

WORD SEARCH

Look at the word list.
Circle the words in the puzzle.

```
P  I  C  T  U  R  E  V  U  T  M
I  S  F  A  E  Q  H  L  E  D  G
L  C  K  B  A  T  H  T  U  B  Z
L  A  T  L  J  D  B  C  L  J  E
O  C  J  E  P  Y  B  O  O  K  Q
W  Z  F  B  A  V  Z  I  F  N  G
K  R  S  P  I  O  V  E  N  U  S
I  S  O  A  P  X  N  K  G  R  I
Y  W  U  O  O  B  Q  R  M  W  N
L  A  M  P  R  E  A  U  X  L  K
V  B  P  H  M  D  S  G  O  H  N
```

SOAP

MATCHING

Find and circle the picture that looks exactly like this one:

© School Zone Publishing 06339

CROSSWORD

Use the clues to fill in the puzzle.

Across

1. The stack of ___ fell down.
3. I lost the sail to my new___.
4. Keisha likes to dress her ___ in jeans.

Down

2. The ___ flew into a tree.
3. The ___ rolled under the chair.
4. A ___ makes a booming sound.

© School Zone Publishing 06339

COLORING

Color the picture.

- ● = red
- ● = blue
- ● = green
- ● = orange
- ● = violet
- ● = brown

DOT-TO-DOT

Connect the dots from 1-30.
Color the picture.

GREEN

BLUE

3   2

4   1

5

8   6

9   7

10   11   12

16   13

14   27

17   15   26

18   19   20   28   29

22   25   30

23   21

24

74

DRAWING PUZZLE

Copy the drawing from each puzzle piece
to its matching place in the grid below.
Trace the dotted lines.
Color the picture.

© School Zone Publishing 06339

PATTERNS

Circle the pictures to complete the patterns.

LEARN TO DRAW

Follow the sample picture in the grid on the top to draw the picture below. Color the picture.

COUNT BY TENS

Draw a line through the maze from start to finish. Start at **10** and count by **tens**.

Start

10	30	10	70	80	90
50	40	20	60	70	40
60	50	30	40	90	60
70	80	70	50	60	70
80	90	30	40	50	80
20	10	20	30	100	90

Finish

CROSSWORD

Use the clues to fill in the puzzle.

| mouse | block | spin |
| bake | sack | nest |

Across
2. It rhymes with "lake."
3. It rhymes with "back."
4. It rhymes with "best."

Down
1. It rhymes with "house."
2. It rhymes with "clock."
3. It rhymes with "twin."

WHAT'S DIFFERENT?

Find and circle **6** things that are different in **picture A** and **picture B**.

Picture A

Picture B

FIGURE IT OUT

Use the clues to solve the problems.

$2 +$ $= 4$

$= \underline{\hspace{3cm}}$

$+$ $= 10$

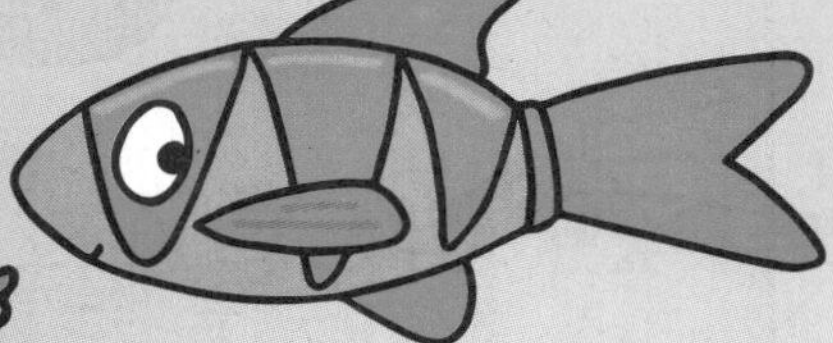

$= \underline{\hspace{3cm}}$

HODGEPODGE

Each  has one that looks exactly like it.
Draw a line between each of the matching pairs.

SOLVE THE CODE

Use the code to solve the riddle.

CODE

	1	2	3	4	5	6
★	O	T	J	L	U	B
◯	U	Q	P	B	L	B
△	R	S	K	O	A	D
●	B	P	L	I	Z	X
▢	N	M	A	H	E	B

What is easy to get into, but hard to get out of?

2 ★ 1 △ 4 △ 5 ★ 6 ◯ 3 ◯ 5 ▢

_ _ _ _ _ _ _

WORD SEARCH

Look at the word list.
Circle the words in the puzzle.

COAT	SHOES
DRESS	SKIRT
GLOVES	SOCKS
JEANS	SWEATER
PANTS	TIGHTS
SHIRT	

```
S W E A T E R B J
K R A R P D Q U E U
I N S Y V A C O A T
R S H O E S I L N I
T H I J S O C K S G
L K R C A K Y D P H
W O T Z F P U B D T
H B G I E A E H R S
F X T L S N J V E Q
L N K G M T J A S I
G L O V E S D R S C
```

WHAT'S DIFFERENT?

Find and circle **6** things that are different in **picture A** and **picture B**.

Picture A

Picture B

MATCHING

Find and circle the picture that looks exactly like this one:

WHAT'S DIFFERENT?

Find and circle **6** things that are different in **picture A** and **picture B**.

Picture A

Picture B

MAZE

Draw a line from start to finish.

START

FINISH

PATTERNS

Color the picture to finish each pattern.

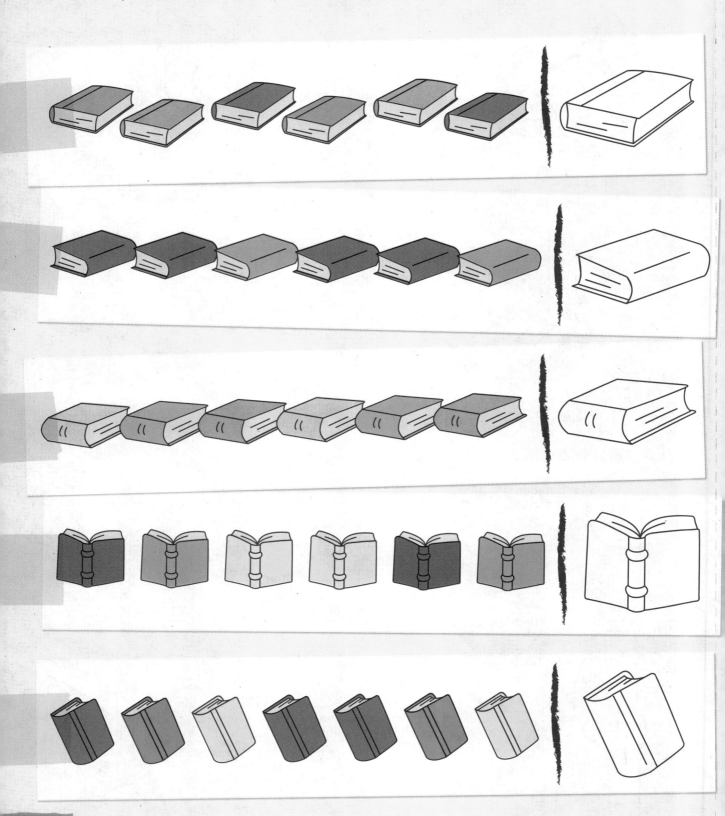

DOT-TO-DOT

Connect the dots from 1-30.
Color the picture.

LEARN TO DRAW

Follow the steps to draw a horse.
Color the picture.

STEP 1:

STEP 2:

STEP 3:

STEP 4:

STEP 5:

STEP 6:

MAZE

Draw a line from start to finish.

START

FINISH

WHAT'S DIFFERENT?

Find and circle **6** things that are different in **picture A** and **picture B**.

Picture A

Picture B

WORD SEARCH

Look at the word list.
Circle the words in the puzzle.

WORD LIST
BALL
DOLL
CARDS
KITE
PUZZLE
ROBOT
BLOCKS

```
R  T  M  G  R  Y  N  B  S
I  K  I  T  E  J  Z  A  Q
X  R  S  B  U  D  O  L  L
L  C  A  R  D  S  W  L  N
M  Q  L  B  F  K  A  E  P
A  H  R  W  Z  H  V  C  U
B  L  O  C  K  S  O  A  Z
Y  P  B  M  D  B  U  T  Z
C  X  O  J  B  U  D  F  L
G  E  T  P  K  V  I  O  E
```

WHAT DO YOU KNOW?

Read each sentence.
Circle **true** or **false**.

1. There are five kids below.

   true   **false**

2. Two of the kids are wearing glasses.

   true   **false**

3. Four of the kids are wearing shoes.

   true   **false**

4. One kid is wearing a hat.

   true   **false**

5. Two of the kids are wearing a green shirt.

   true   **false**

6. One kid is wearing a yellow dress.

   true   **false**

WHAT'S DIFFERENT?

Find and circle **6** things that are different in **picture A** and **picture B**.

Picture A

Picture B

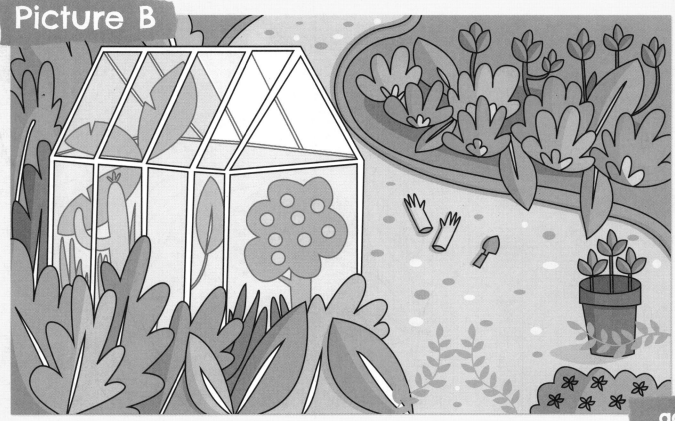

SEARCH

Look at the picture and write how many of each you can find.

snails

grasshoppers

bee

spiders

dragonflies

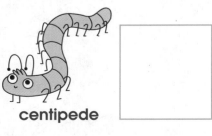
centipede

COLORING

Color the picture.

● = red
● = blue
● = green
● = orange
● = purple
● = black

MISSING PUZZLE PIECES

Draw a line from each puzzle piece to its place in the puzzle.

WHAT'S DIFFERENT?

Find and circle **6** things that are different in **picture A** and **picture B**.

Picture A

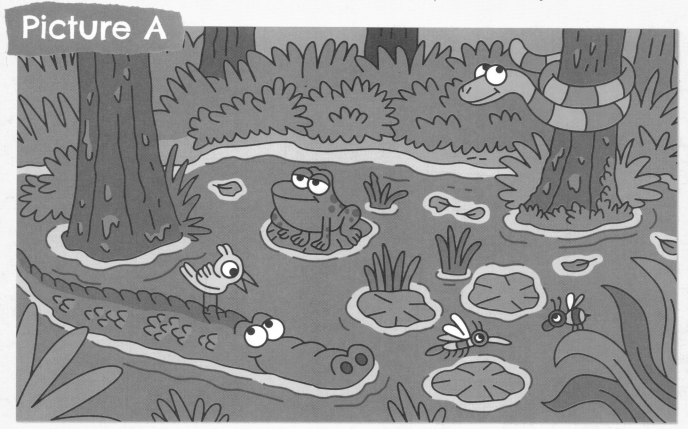

Picture B

SOLVE THE CODE

Use the code to solve the riddle.

CODE

	1	2	3	4	5	6
☆	O	I	Y	W	L	R
⬭	R	E	D	B	G	C
▲	K	X	F	D	H	J
●	L	A	C	K	S	M
◼	M	Q	O	N	T	R

Which month has 28 days?

2   5   1   1   3   5   5   2   6

___ ___ ___   ___ ___ ___ ___ ___ ___

SOLVE THE CODE

Follow the directions.
Then read the message that is left.

Color the **J** boxes red.
Color the **Q** boxes blue.
Color the **X** boxes green.
Color the **Z** boxes yellow.

J	Q	H	O	W	Z	M	A	N	Y
Z	X	I	N	C	H	E	S	Q	J
X	A	R	E	Z	X	I	N	J	X
Q	Z	A	J	Q	F	O	O	T	?

Write the hidden message. Then answer the question.

_____

_____

WORD SEARCH

Look at the word list.
Circle the words in the puzzle.

```
T  E  B  Q  X  P  O  T  A  T  O  D
O  R  A  N  G  E  L  N  J  R  Z  Y
M  D  N  S  Y  A  P  R  I  C  O  T
A  C  A  L  O  R  W  E  M  A  I  S
T  Q  N  C  H  W  O  L  A  R  A  P
O  C  A  P  P  L  E  A  J  R  Z  M
V  P  T  K  D  B  B  F  C  O  R  N
C  H  E  R  R  Y  K  T  U  T  Z  I
U  N  B  E  R  A  F  H  V  O  Q  F
Y  T  I  P  U  M  P  K  I  N  Y  N
J  G  V  U  N  G  S  Z  G  M  H  K
```

WORD LIST

APPLE	PEAR
APRICOT	POTATO
BANANA	PUMPKIN
CARROT	TOMATO
CHERRY	YAM
CORN	ORANGE

MATCHING

Find and circle the picture that looks exactly like this one:

CROSSWORD

Use the clues to fill in the puzzle.

Across
2. I rhyme with slip.

4. I rhyme with rain.

5. I rhyme with star.

Down
1. I rhyme with us.

3. I rhyme with drain.

4. I rhyme with duck.

WHAT'S DIFFERENT?

Find and circle **6** things that are different in **picture A** and **picture B**.

Picture A

Picture B

SEARCH & FIND

Look at the picture and write how many of each you can find.

 snakes
 frogs
 woodpecker
 turtles

LEARN TO DRAW

Follow the sample picture in the grid to draw the picture below.
Color the picture.

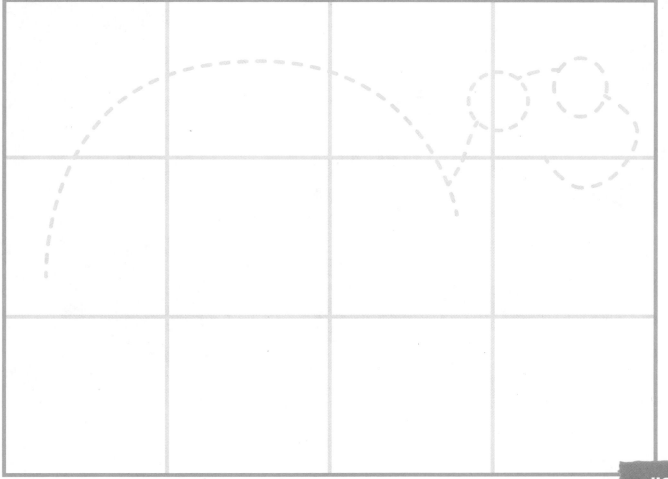

MAZE

Draw a line from start to finish.

START

FINISH

WHAT'S DIFFERENT?

Find and circle **6** things that are different in **picture A** and **picture B**.

Picture A

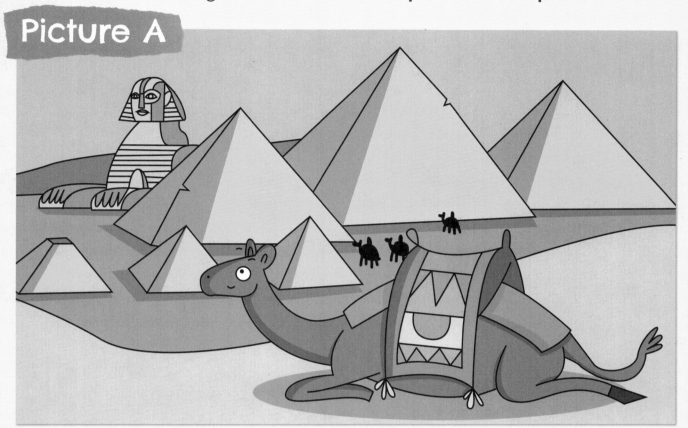

Picture B

LEARN TO DRAW

Follow the steps to draw a cat.
Color the picture.

STEP 1:

STEP 2:

STEP 3:

STEP 4:

STEP 5:

STEP 6:

SEARCH

Look at the picture and write how many of each you can find.

drums

toy car

toy boats

toy soldiers

yo-yos

jack-in-the-box

DOT-TO-DOT

Connect the dots from 1-30.
Color the picture.

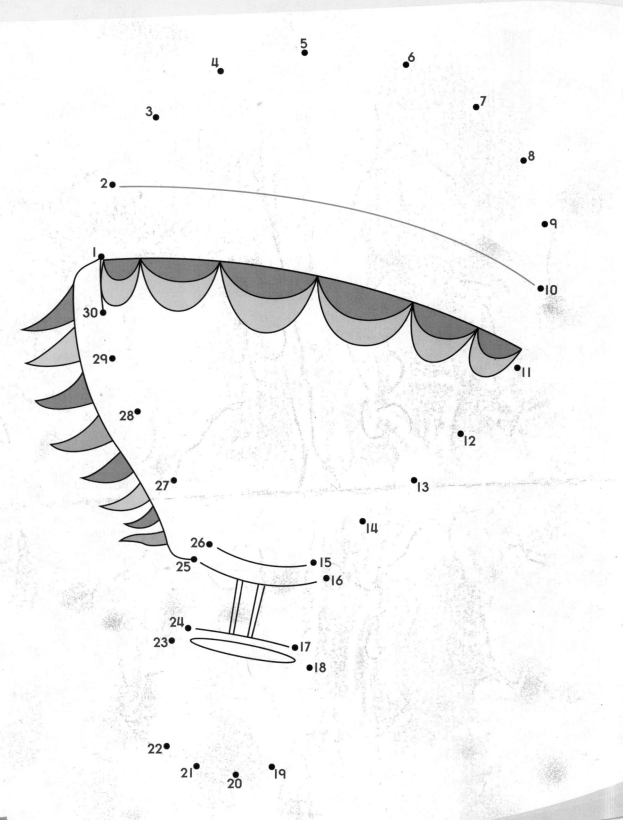

© School Zone Publishing 06339

PATTERNS

Color the picture to complete each pattern.

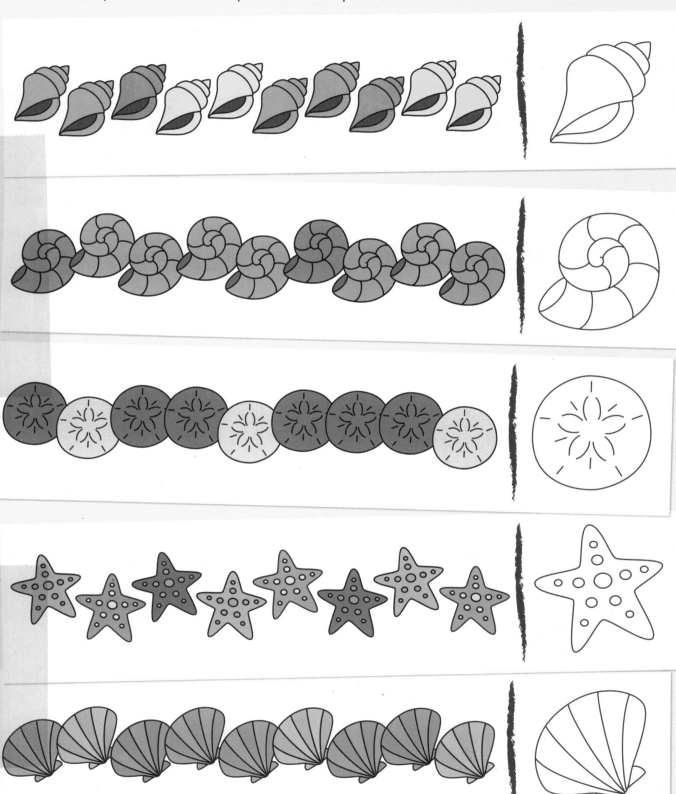

SOLVE THE CODE

Look at the pictures.
Write the names of the pictures in their numbered rows in the puzzle.
Use the code to solve the riddle.

1. **comets**   2. **sun**   3. **planets**   4. **moon**   5. **stars**

What is another name for an astronaut?

5   1   4   5   4   4   3   5   2   3

___ ___ ___ ___ ___ ___ ___ ___ ___ ___

WHAT'S DIFFERENT?

Find and circle **6** things that are different in **picture A** and **picture B**.

Picture A

Picture B

MATCHING

Find and circle the picture that looks exactly like this one:

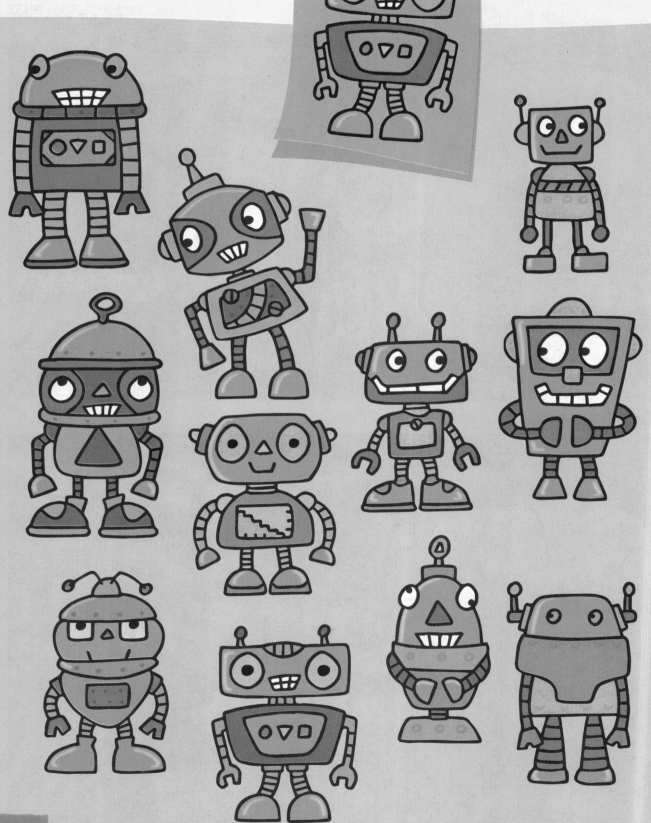

FIGURE IT OUT

Use the clues to solve the problems.

apple $+ 3 = 9$

apple $=$ _____

bee $+$ apple $= 14$

bee $=$ _____

bee $- 4 =$ _____

HODGEPODGE

Each  has one that looks exactly like it.
Draw a line between each of the matching pairs.

WHAT'S DIFFERENT?

Find and circle **6** things that are different in **picture A** and **picture B**.

Picture A

Picture B

CROSSWORD

Use the clues to fill in the puzzle.

Across

2. It is a ___ day, so I am going to the beach.
4. A cloud near the ground makes it ___.
5. I use an umbrella when it is ___.

Down

1. Things blow away when it is ___.
2. I wear a hat and mittens when it is ___.
3. You can't see the sun when it is ___.

© School Zone Publishing 06339

MATCHING

Find and circle the picture that looks exactly like this one:

WHAT'S DIFFERENT?

Find and circle **6** things that are different in **picture A** and **picture B**.

Picture A

Picture B

COLORING

Color the picture.

- ● = red
- ● = blue
- ● = green
- ● = orange
- ● = purple
- ● = black

© School Zone Publishing 06339

SEARCH

Look at the picture and write how many of each you can find.

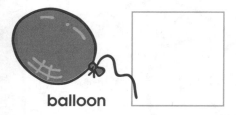

balloon

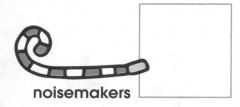

noisemakers

gifts

party hats

pieces of cake

candles

DOT-TO-DOT

Connect the dots from 1-30.
Color the picture.

PATTERNS

Circle the pictures to complete the patterns.

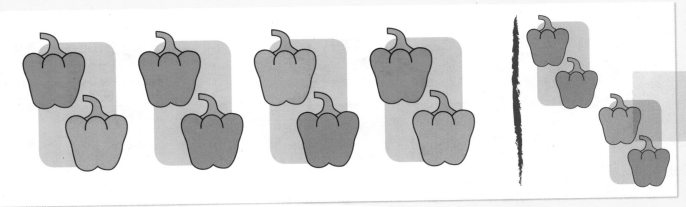

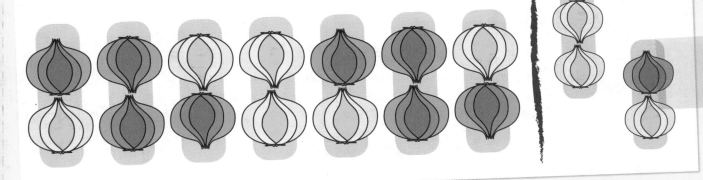

WHAT'S DIFFERENT?

Find and circle **6** things that are different in **picture A** and **picture B**.

Picture A

Picture B

Use the code to solve the riddle.

CODE

	1	2	3	4	5	6	7
■ (gray square)	Y	W	N	R	Z	N	H
★ (star)	K	F	P	Q	M	E	Z
⬭ (oval)	B	J	I	M	I	K	N
▲ (triangle)	N	C	W	Q	G	R	I
● (circle)	S	Y	N	F	P	U	L
◻ (square)	A	B	K	S	I	U	W

Which nail doesn't a carpenter like to hit?

1   2   5   3   5   6   4   7   1   3   7

(square) (star) (oval) (circle) (triangle) (star) (square) (oval) (square) (oval) (circle)

___ ___ ___ ___ ___ ___ ___ ___ ___ ___ ___

WORD SEARCH

Look at the word list.
Circle the words in the puzzle.

COW
CHICKEN
DUCK
FARMER
GOAT
GOOSE
HORSE
LAMB
SHEEP
TRACTOR
TURKEY

```
C O W I T U R K E Y
H W S E R A F Q F N
I J G O A T E A W X
C I O M C P D U C K
K H E Z T V G R G D
E U P H O R S E F S
N Y B O R Y Q R D H
B H S A Z T D L J E
F A R M E R K A B E
V M N U K C T M X P
L G O O S E C B C L
```

140

© School Zone Publishing 06339

WHAT DO YOU KNOW?

Read each sentence.
Circle **true** or **false**.

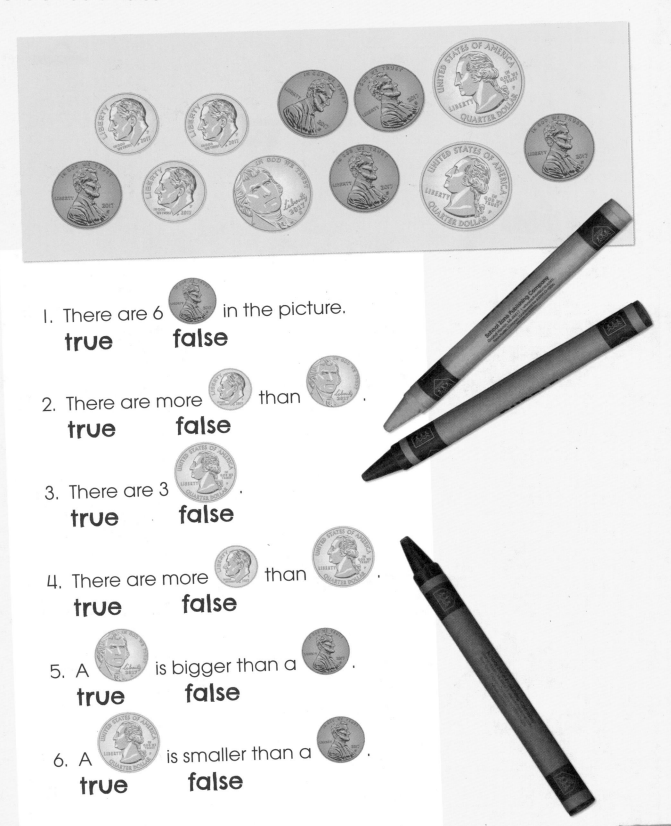

1. There are 6 in the picture.

   true   **false**

2. There are more than .

   true   **false**

3. There are 3 .

   true   **false**

4. There are more than .

   true   **false**

5. A is bigger than a .

   true   **false**

6. A is smaller than a .

   true   **false**

WHAT'S DIFFERENT?

Find and circle **6** things that are different in **picture A** and **picture B**.

Picture A

Picture B

142

MATCHING

Find and circle the picture that looks exactly like this one:

HODGEPODGE

Each  has one that looks exactly like it.
Draw a line between each of the matching pairs.

144

DOT-TO-DOT

Connect the dots from 1-30.
Color the picture.

PATTERNS

Circle the pictures to complete the patterns.

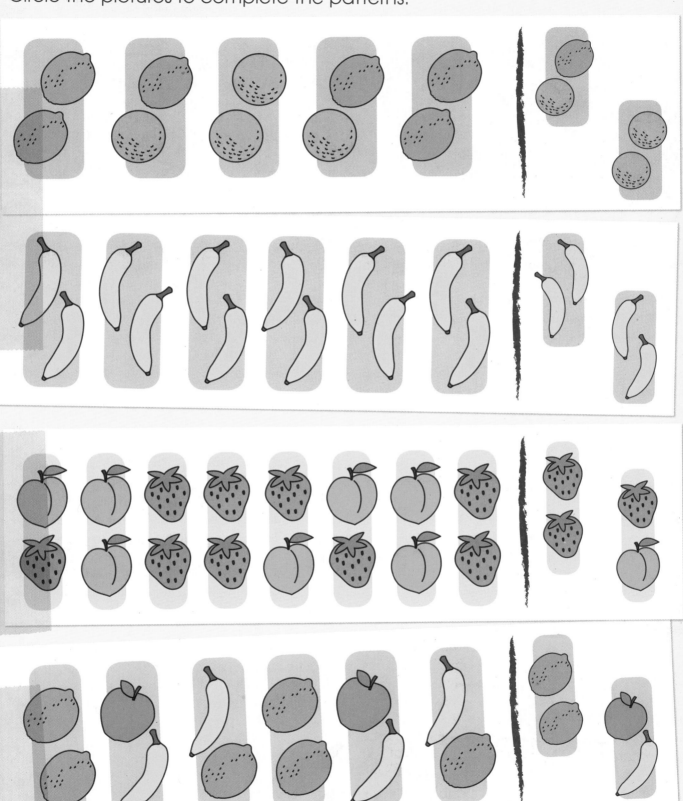

© School Zone Publishing 06339

LEARN TO DRAW

Follow the steps to draw a car.
Color the picture.

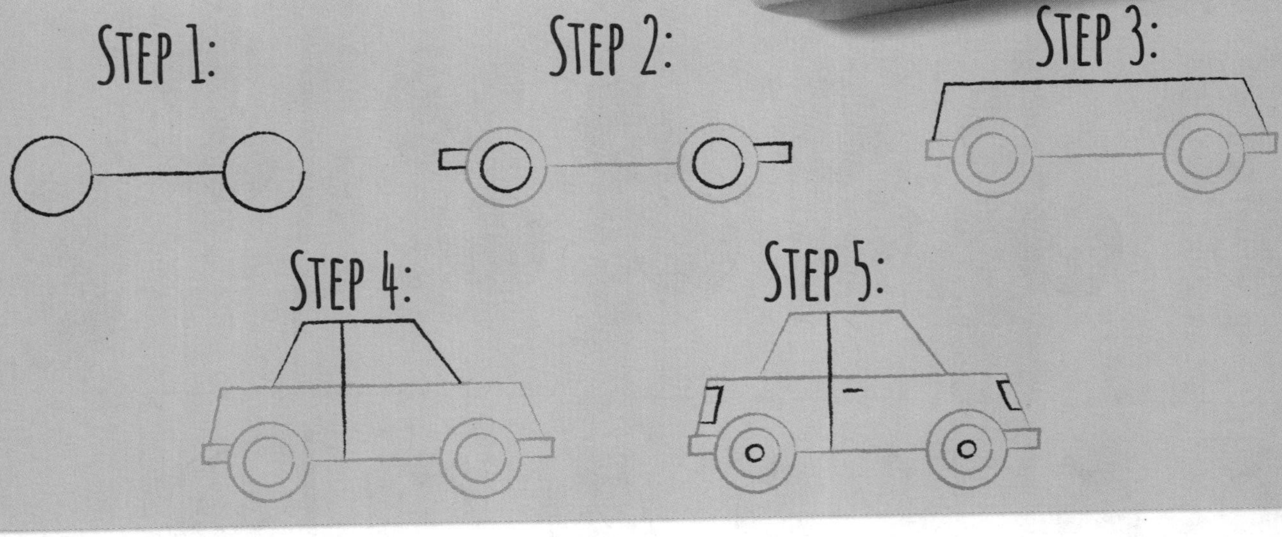

Step 1:

Step 2:

Step 3:

Step 4:

Step 5:

148

SEARCH & FIND

Look at the picture and write how many of each you can find.

 **rattlesnakes**

 **toads**

 **lizards**

 **vulture**

MAZE

Draw a line from start to finish.

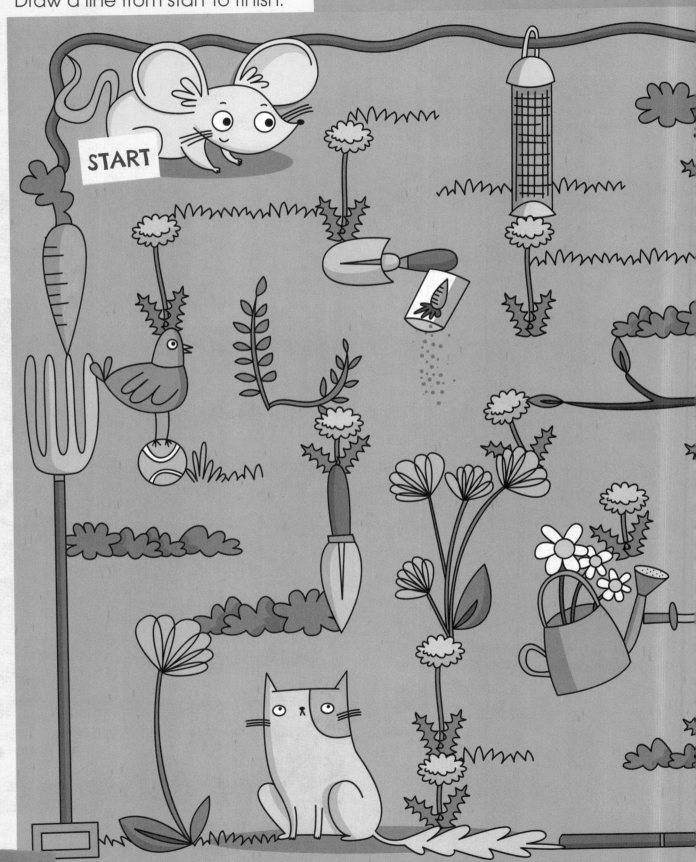

START

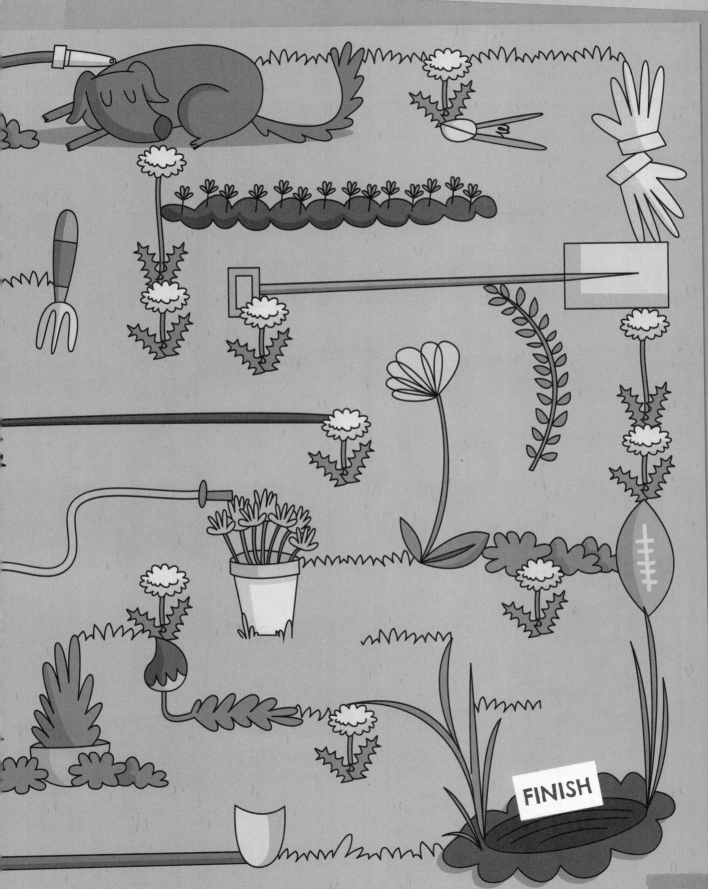

FINISH

MISSING PUZZLE PIECES

Draw a line from each puzzle piece to its place in the puzzle.

CROSSWORD

Use the clues to fill in the puzzle.

WORD LIST

| old | down | slow |
| short | night | near |

Across

1. The opposite of new is ___.
3. The opposite of fast is ___.
4. The opposite of day is ___.

Down

2. The opposite of up is ___.
3. The opposite of long is ___.
4. The opposite of far is ___.

FINISH

WHAT'S DIFFERENT?

Find and circle **6** things that are different in **picture A** and **picture B**.

Picture A

Picture B

SOLVE THE CODE

Why are fish so smart?
Follow the directions.
Then read the message that is left.

Color the **K** boxes green.
Color the **V** boxes red.
Color the **X** boxes blue.
Color the **P** boxes orange.

X	V	T	H	E	Y	P	G	O	V	P
V	P	X	K	V	P	X	V	P	K	x
P	X	A	R	O	U	N	D	V	X	P
K	V	K	X	V	V	K	X	P	V	K
I	N	P	S	C	H	O	O	L	S	.

Write the answer to the riddle.

_____

_____

SOLVE THE CODE

Use the code to solve the riddle.

CODE

▬	Y	U	R	N	N	E	I
★	M	J	B	Z	J	A	P
⬭	G	L	L	T	Q	C	B
▲	B	A	H	P	K	I	K
●	S	G	S	S	D	O	R
◼	Q	L	B	D	V	N	U
	1	2	3	4	5	6	7

Which kind of insect sleeps the most?

2   3   6   5   7   2   1

▲   ◼   ◼   ●   ⬭   ◼   ⬭

____ ____ ____ ____ ____ ____ ____

WHAT'S DIFFERENT?

Find and circle **6** things that are different in **picture A** and **picture B**.

Picture A

Picture B

MAZE

Draw a line from start to finish.

FINISH

START

PATTERNS

Circle the pictures to complete the patterns.

HODGEPODGE

Each  has one that looks exactly like it.
Draw a line between each of the matching pairs.

160

HIDDEN PICTURE

YARD SALE

Find and circle the hidden pictures.

tree

rocket

star

bone

envelope

banana

cupcake

ship

feather

candle

WORD SCRAMBLE

How many words can you make from the letters in **YARD SALE** ?

1. _____

2. _____

3. _____

4. _____

5. _____

6. _____

7. _____

8. _____

9. _____

10. _____

11. _____

12. _____

5 = GOOD   8 = GREAT   12 = BRILLIANT!

DOT-TO-DOT

Connect the dots from 1-30.
Color the picture.

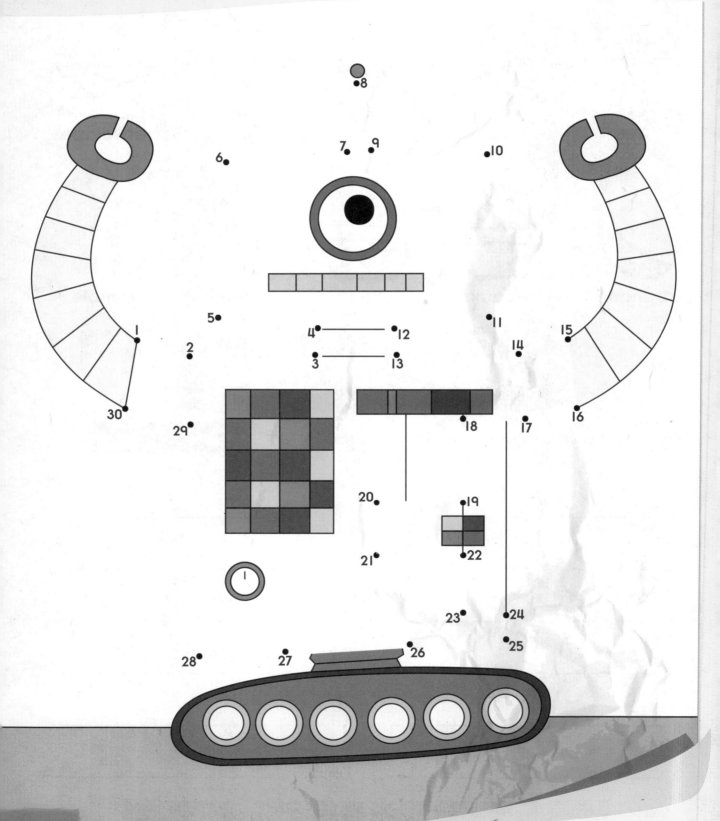

CROSSWORD

Use the clues to fill in the puzzle.

Across

2. Is your answer ___?
4. Put the book over ___.
5. The store is having a ___ on shoes.

Down

1. Can you ___ your name?
3. They like ___ new home.
5. Where did you ___ your new boat?

WHAT'S DIFFERENT?

Find and circle **6** things that are different in **picture A** and **picture B**.

Picture A

Picture B

166

WHAT DO YOU KNOW?

Read each sentence.
Circle **true** or **false**.

1. Butterflies have wings.
   true   **false**

2. There are three butterflies.
   true   **false**

3. Two of the butterflies are green.
   true   **false**

4. The orange butterfly is in the middle.
   true   **false**

5. The purple butterfly is smaller than the green butterfly.
   true   **false**

6. The pink butterfly is the largest butterfly.
   true   **false**

LEARN TO DRAW

Follow the steps to draw a monkey.
Color the picture.

STEP 1:

STEP 2:

STEP 3:

STEP 4:

STEP 5:

STEP 6:

MISSING PUZZLE PIECES

Draw a line from each puzzle piece to its place in the puzzle.

MAZE

Help the monkey get to the ground.

DOT-TO-DOT

Connect the dots from 1-30.
Color the picture.

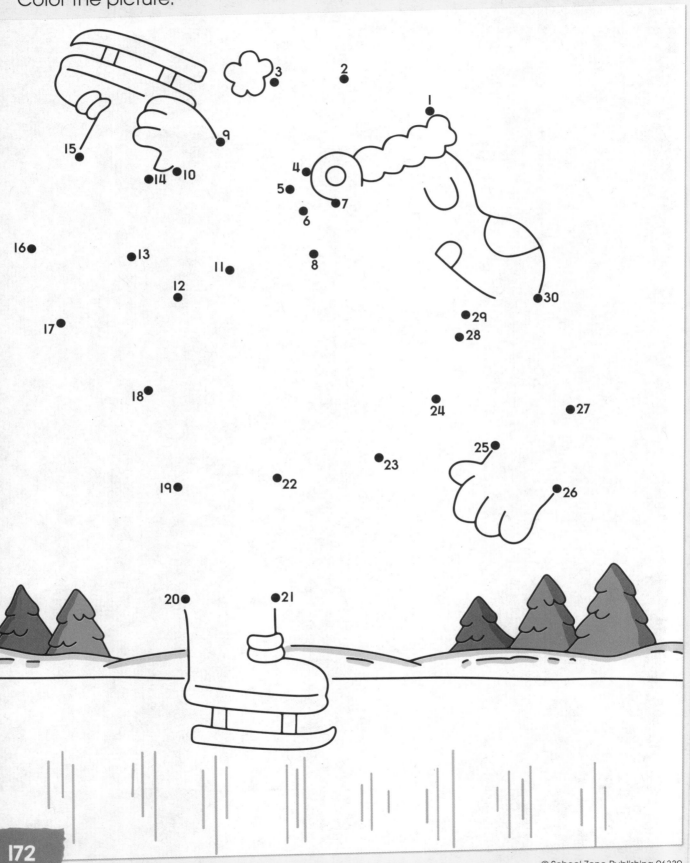

WHAT'S DIFFERENT?

Find and circle **6** things that are different in **picture A** and **picture B**.

Picture A

Picture B

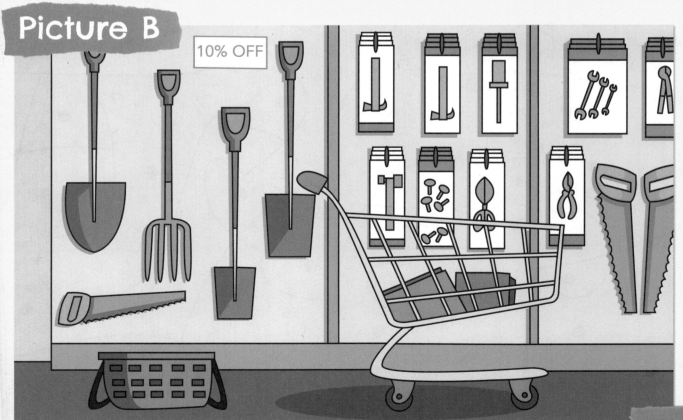

COLORING

Color the picture.

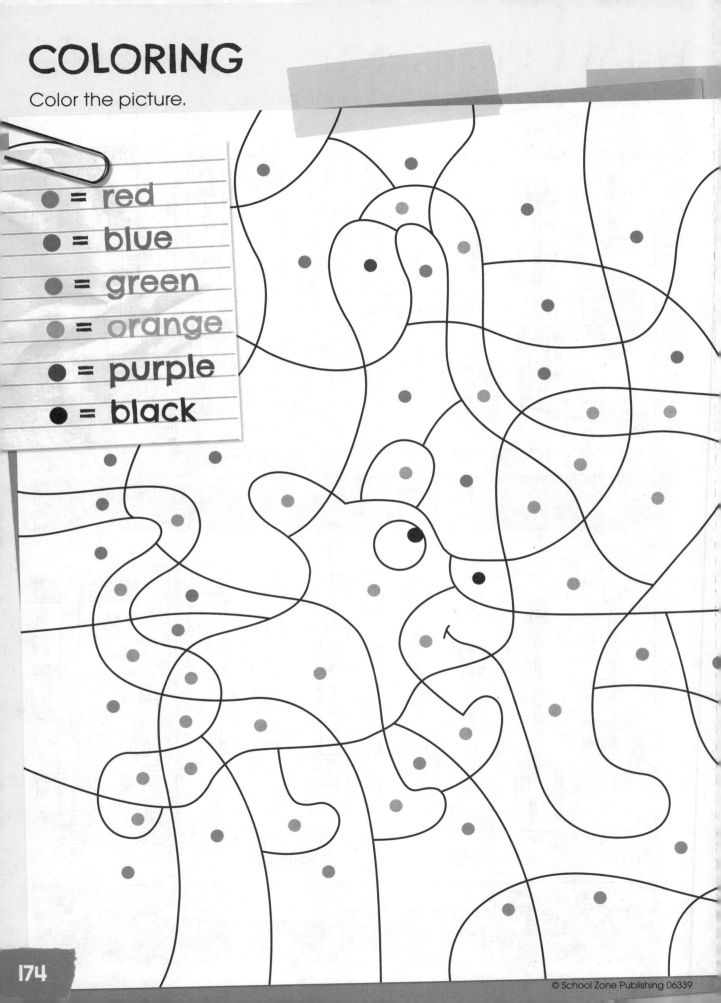

- ● = red
- ● = blue
- ● = green
- ● = orange
- ● = purple
- ● = black

174

HIDDEN PICTURE

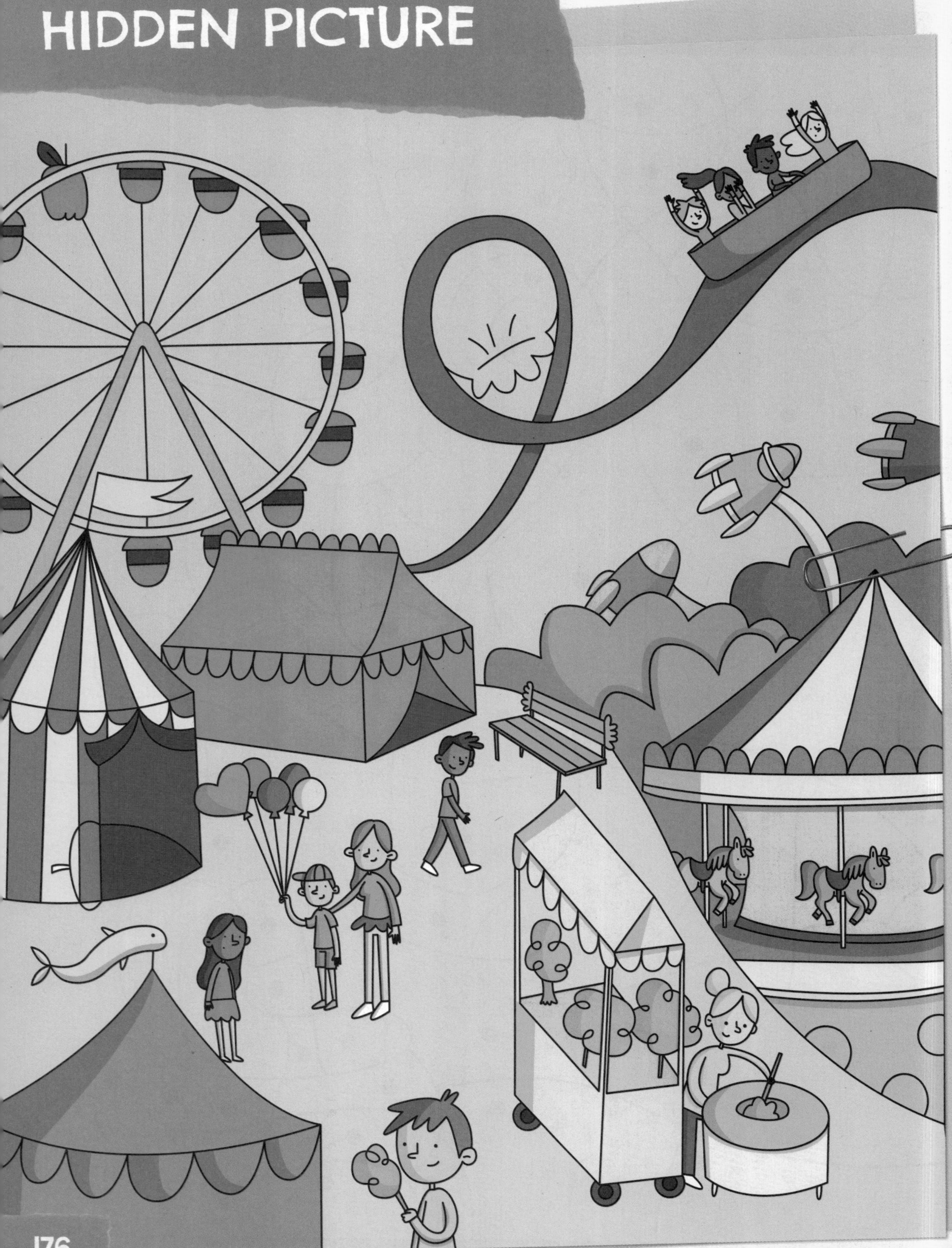

Find and circle the hidden pictures.

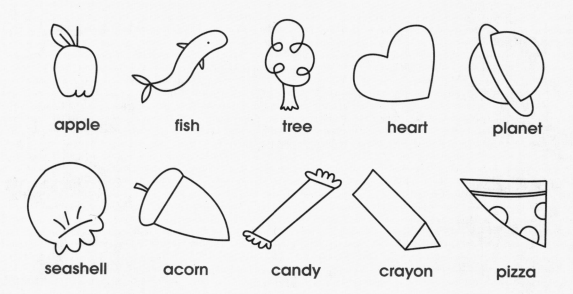

apple   fish   tree   heart   planet

seashell   acorn   candy   crayon   pizza

WORD SCRAMBLE

How many words can you make from the letters in AMUSEMENT ?

1. _____   8. _____

2. _____   9. _____

3. _____   10. _____

4. _____   11. _____

5. _____   12. _____

6. _____   13. _____

7. _____   14. _____

6 = GOOD   10 = GREAT   14 = BRILLIANT!

WHAT'S DIFFERENT?

Find and circle **6** things that are different in **picture A** and **picture B**.

Picture A

Picture B

SOLVE THE CODE

Use the code to solve the riddle.

CODE

	1	2	3	4	5	6
★	T	S	Y	A	M	W
⬭	I	L	Q	D	H	K
△	U	Z	R	P	E	I
○	T	U	C	Y	N	P
▢	E	P	T	R	R	Y

What key will not open a door?

4   1   2   3   6   1   6

___ ___ ___ ___ ___ ___ ___

WORD SEARCH

Look at the word list.
Circle the words in the puzzle.

WORD LIST

- AIRPLANE
- BOAT
- CAR
- DIGGER
- ROCKET
- SCOOTER
- TANKER
- TAXI
- TRAIN
- TRUCK
- VAN

```
C T R A I N Q L B H
P R F R K S W M O P
A U G R F F B N A G
S C O O T E R O T A
Q K X C R B E I V I
D J D K J C A R Z R
I S O E C L U L H P
G A U T A X I V H L
G D E Y Z I T D X A
E N K C M T Y V A N
R V T A N K E R W E
```

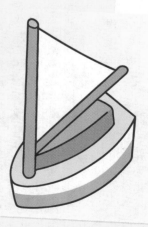

WHAT DO YOU KNOW?

Read each sentence.
Circle **true** or **false**.

1. There are 3 kids in the picture.
   true   **false**

2. The boy is wearing a hat.
   true   **false**

3. The girl is holding up the number 4.
   true   **false**

4. The sky is pink.
   true   **false**

5. The girl has purple spots on her dress.
   true   **false**

6. The fence is yellow.
   true   **false**

WHAT'S DIFFERENT?

Find and circle **6** things that are different in **picture A** and **picture B**.

Picture A

Picture B

MATCHING

Find and circle the picture that looks exactly like this one:

CROSSWORD

Use the clues to fill in the puzzle.

Across

1. I am also the name of a color.
3. I am long and yellow.
5. I rhyme with "bear."
6. I am used to make a tart drink.

Down

2. I grow in bunches.
4. Would you like a slice of ___ pie?

WORD LIST

orange   pear   banana
grapes   lemon   apple

MAZE

Draw a line from start to finish.

START

FINISH

COLORING

Color the picture.

- ● = red
- ● = blue
- ● = green
- ● = orange
- ● = purple
- ● = pink

PATTERNS

Circle the pictures to complete the patterns.

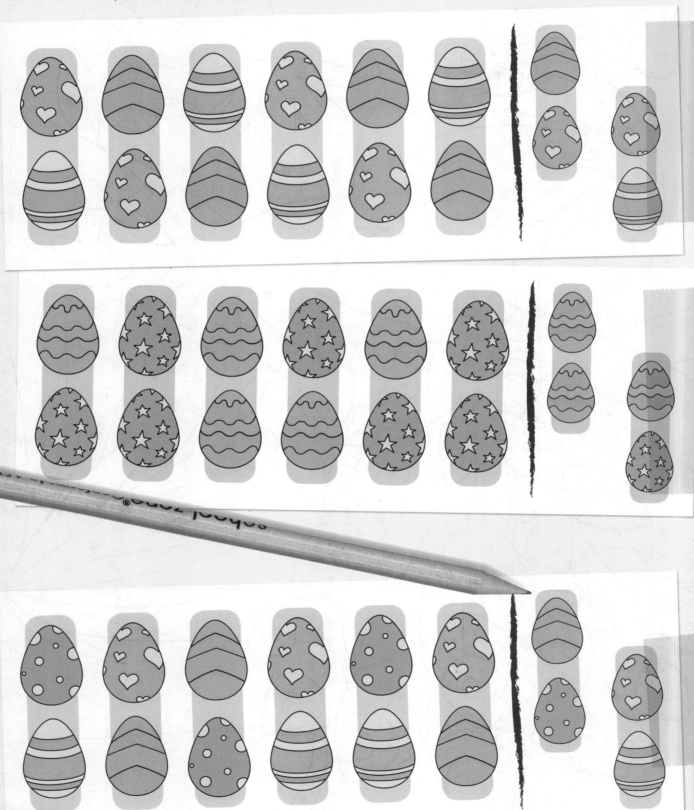

DOT-TO-DOT

Connect the dots from 1-35.
Color the picture.

WHAT'S DIFFERENT?

Find and circle **6** things that are different in **picture A** and **picture B**.

Picture A

Picture B

190

SOLVE THE CODE

Use the code to solve the riddle.

CODE

★	T	S	Y	R	M	W
⬭	I	L	S	D	H	A
▲	U	W	E	P	X	I
⬤	T	V	C	Y	N	P
◼	K	P	T	E	R	X
	1	2	3	4	5	6

What kind of shoes do spies wear?

2   5   3   6   1   4   4   3

___ ___ ___ ___ ___ ___ ___ ___

WHAT DO YOU KNOW?

Read each sentence.
Circle **true** or **false**.

1. All of the mice are blue.
   true   **false**

2. The mice have pink tails.
   true   **false**

3. There are five mice.
   true   **false**

4. The sun is yellow.
   true   **false**

5. The water is blue.
   true   **false**

6. The land is orange.
   true   **false**

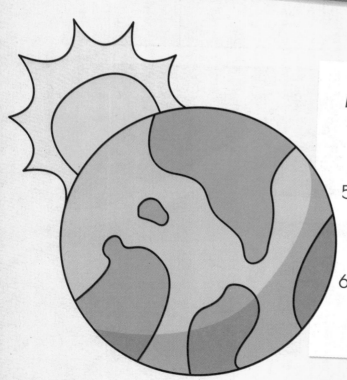

MATCHING

Find and circle the picture that looks exactly like this one:

SEARCH

Look at the picture and write how many of each you can find.

bananas

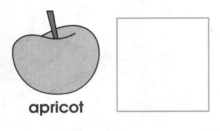

apricot

apples

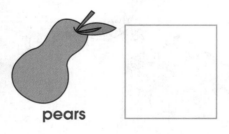

pears

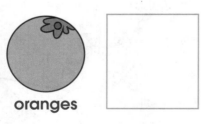

oranges

peaches

194

MAZE

Draw a line from start to finish.

START

FINISH

DOT-TO-DOT

Connect the dots from 1-35.
Color the picture.

WHAT'S DIFFERENT?

Find and circle **6** things that are different in **picture A** and **picture B**.

Picture A

Picture B

SOLVE THE CODE

Use the code to solve the riddle.

CODE

a	j	g
i	u	e
b	r	t

What do you call a dancing beetle?

WORD SEARCH

Look at the word list.
Circle the words in the puzzle.

WORD LIST

CAT	PUMPKIN
GHOST	SPIDER
GOBLIN	WEB
MASK	BAT
MOON	

```
J S H Q W P U M P K I N J E
W A F A W C W G H O S T W S
S F V H U W R F P L X G H N
P N A K C N W S W B A T J W
I M Y M O Q T W T X C M K L
D X D N T L P E W M X J V E
E S Y Z B R A V D W M W X B
R Z C G O G W N W H L E L O
W V P H L M Q D T Y O W S N
E N R C B W B P Q E O U N R
B W N B X K W I V W R W S P
G O B L I N V F E G H N L E
M O O N K M A S K W C A T I
```

MATCHING

Find and circle the picture that
looks exactly like this one:

LEARN TO DRAW

Follow the steps to draw a bear.
Color the picture.

STEP 1: STEP 2: STEP 3: STEP 4: STEP 5:

HODGEPODGE

Each  has one that looks exactly like it.
Draw a line between each of the matching pairs.

DOT-TO-DOT

Connect the dots from 1-40.
Color the picture.

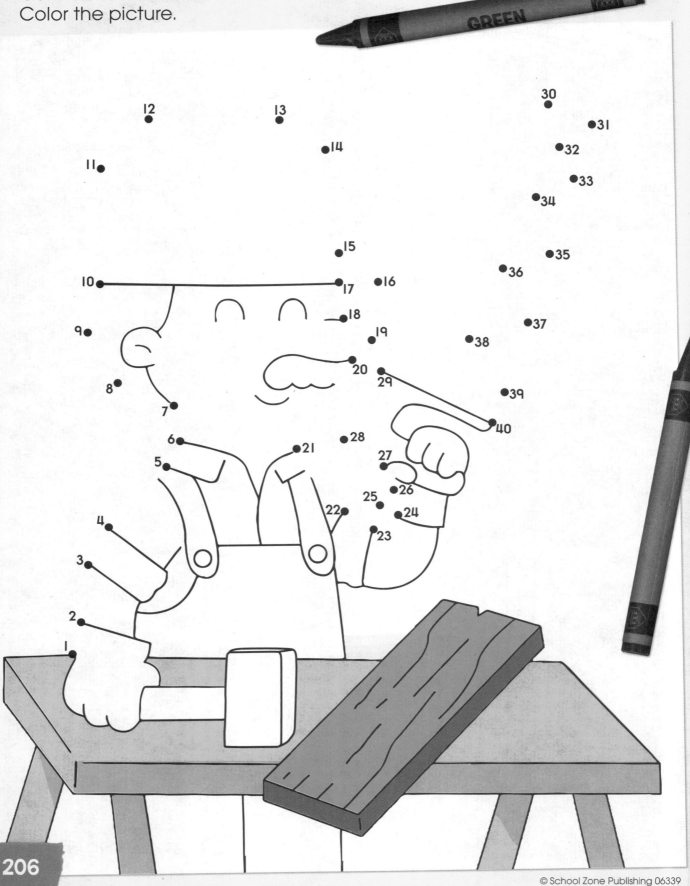

WHAT DO YOU KNOW?

Read each sentence.
Circle **true** or **false**.

1. The dog in the picture has a blue collar.
   true   **false**

2. The dog has brown fur.
   true   **false**

3. There are three cats in the picture.
   true   **false**

4. The red cat is smaller than the dog.
   true   **false**

5. There are more cats in the picture than dogs.
   true   **false**

6. Dogs meow and cats bark.
   true   **false**

Find and circle the hidden pictures.

hand rake   spray bottle   glove   hose   watering can

plant food   shovel   clippers   hat   boot

WORD SCRAMBLE

How many words can you make from the letters in **GREENHOUSE** ?

1. _____   8. _____

2. _____   9. _____

3. _____   10. _____

4. _____   11. _____

5. _____   12. _____

6. _____   13. _____

7. _____   14. _____

6 = GOOD   10 = GREAT   14 = BRILLIANT!

PATTERNS

Circle the pictures to complete the patterns.

WHAT'S DIFFERENT?

Find and circle **6** things that are different in **picture A** and **picture B**.

Picture A

Picture B

Use the code to solve the riddle.

What is a ghost's favorite dessert?

CODE

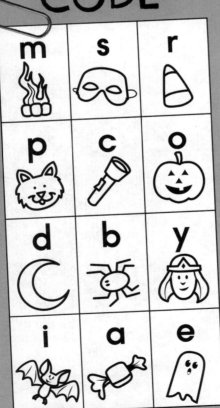

m	s	r
p	c	o
d	b	y
i	a	e

and

!

WORD SEARCH

Find and circle the words in the puzzle.

WORD LIST

bear	monkey
elephant	panda
giraffe	rhino
hippo	tiger
lion	zebra

```
T T A H I P P O K Q
I Q K J K R S A E M
G Z N O X R H I N O
E L E P H A N T L N
R L B J F Q Z D N K
H I V Q E B E A R E
M O X I B C B V J Y
I N X H P I R S F K
V Y M C E P A N D A
G I R A F F E L B M
```

LEARN TO DRAW

Follow the steps to draw a bat.
Color the picture.

STEP 1:   STEP 2:   STEP 3:   STEP 4:

214

STEP 5:

STEP 6:

SEARCH

Look at the picture and write how many of each you can find.

crows

crescent moons

pumpkins

skeleton

black cats

witches hat

216

WHAT'S DIFFERENT?

Find and circle **6** things that are different in **picture A** and **picture B**.

Picture A

Picture B

WORD SEARCH

Use the clues to fill in the puzzle.

WORD LIST

- CATTAIL
- FLY
- FISH
- FROG
- LILYPAD
- POND
- TURTLE
- SWAMP

```
T U R T L E T J C O
F R O G F I S H C O
Q U E O L R P O N D
A B Z K J S W A M P
C R K P E O O K P S
H F X M Q V B Y C F
Z L I L Y P A D A I
I Y C A T T A I L O
G Y I N B X I T R D
B U O M O Z E B D O
```

COLORING

Color the picture.

- ● = pink
- ● = dark blue
- ● = green
- ● = orange
- ● = blue
- ● = brown

WHAT DO YOU KNOW?

Read each sentence.
Circle **true** or **false**.

1. All 3 trophies are gold.
   true   **false**

2. The 1st place trophy is bigger than the 3rd place trophy.
   true   **false**

3. The 2nd place trophy is smaller than the 3rd place trophy.
   true   **false**

4. The 3rd place trophy has a red ribbon on it.
   true   **false**

5. The 2nd place trophy has a star on it.
   true   **false**

6. All of the trophies have a star on them.
   true   **false**

MATCHING

Find and circle the picture that
looks exactly like this one:

COLORING

Color the picture.

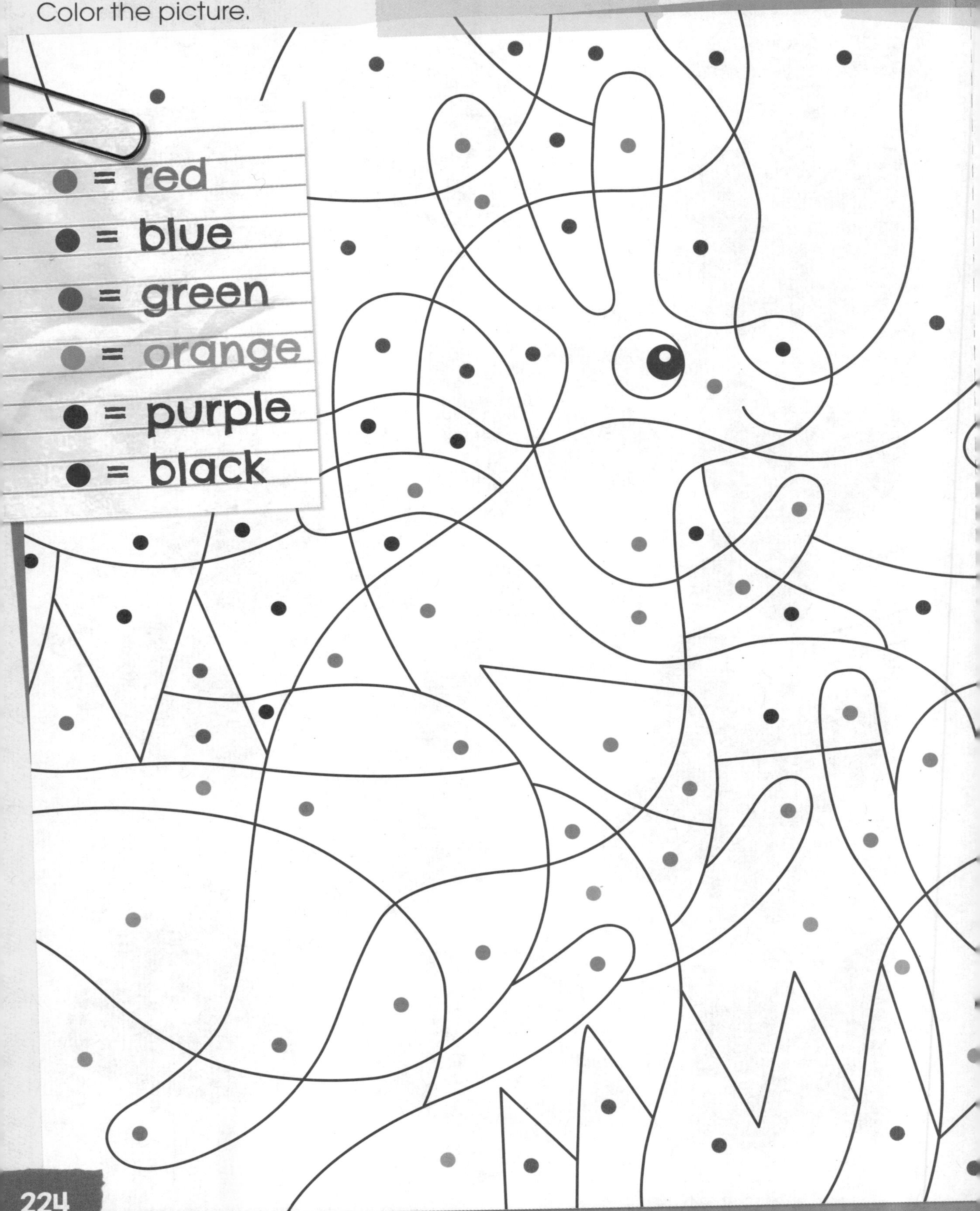

- ● = red
- ● = blue
- ● = green
- ● = orange
- ● = purple
- ● = black

224

MAZE

Draw a line from start to finish.

START

FINISH

SCHOOL

DOT-TO-DOT

Connect the dots from 1-40.
Color the picture.

WHAT DO YOU KNOW?

Read each sentence.
Circle **true** or **false**.

1. There are 3 bananas in the picture.
   true   **false**

2. There are 5 pieces of red fruit.
   true   **false**

3. There is more orange fruit than green fruit.
   true   **false**

4. There are two pieces of green fruit.
   true   **false**

5. There is more red fruit then yellow fruit.
   true   **false**

6. The bowl has 4 pieces of fruit in it.
   true   **false**

FIGURE IT OUT

Use the clues to solve the problems.

❄ + 3 = 12

❄ = _____

❄ + ❄ = 19

❄ = _____

❄ − ❄ = _____

TIC-TAC-TOE

Find the words that go together.
Look across, down, and diagonally.

People

and	pat	red
dad	mom	brother
blue	the	sing

Animals

did	eat	cat
bake	rabbit	do
dog	come	sit

Places

sad	big	school
small	hot	zoo
happy	cold	beach

Things

ball	talk	jump
run	bike	tall
wide	sheep	car

HODGEPODGE

Each  has one that looks exactly like it.
Draw a line between each of the matching pairs.

232

HIDDEN PICTURE

Find and circle the hidden pictures.

ball of
yarn

paintbrush

apple

ice cream
cone

soccer ball

bee

fish

gift

leaf

WORD SCRAMBLE

How many words can you make from the letters in **WARM BREAD**?

1. _____
2. _____
3. _____
4. _____
5. _____
6. _____
7. _____
8. _____
9. _____
10. _____

11. _____
12. _____
13. _____
14. _____
15. _____
16. _____
17. _____
18. _____
19. _____
20. _____

10 = GOOD   15 = GREAT   20 = BRILLIANT!

235

MISSING PUZZLE PIECES

Draw a line from each puzzle piece to its place in the puzzle.

WHAT'S DIFFERENT?

Find and circle **6** things that are different in **picture A** and **picture B**.

Picture A

Picture B

COLORING

Color the picture.

- ● = red
- ● = blue
- ● = green
- ● = orange
- ● = purple
- ● = black

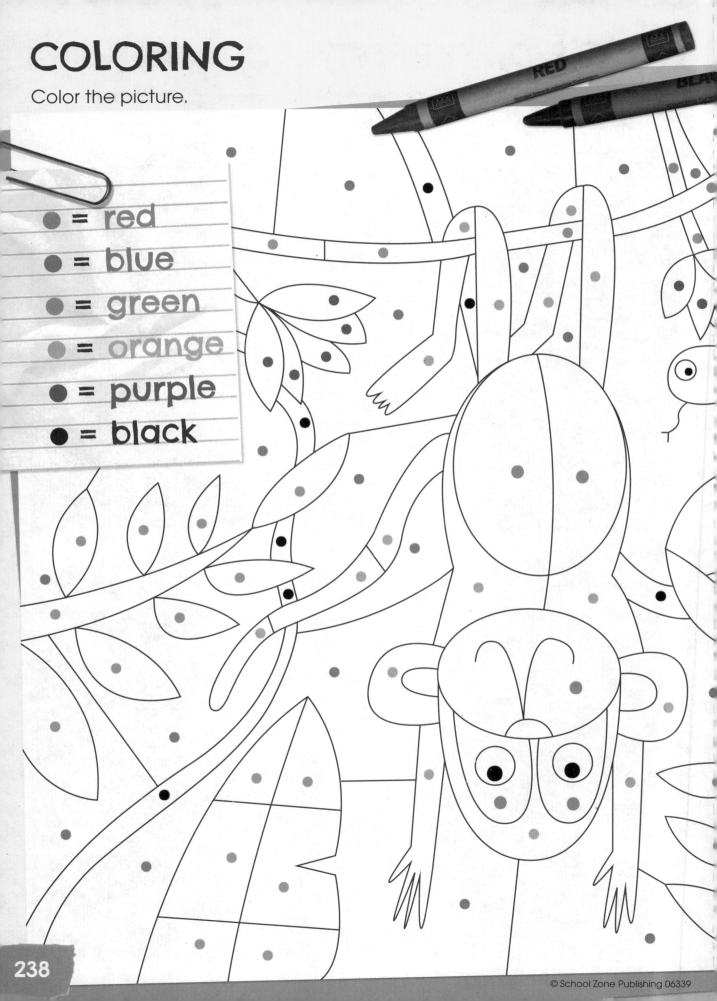

DOT-TO-DOT

Connect the dots from 1-40.
Color the picture.

© School Zone Publishing 06339

WORD SEARCH

Look at the word list.
Circle the words in the puzzle.

```
C O R A L R E E F J
S S X O M V R T Q E
E X W B C M N P O L
A Q V V X Z L V R L
H K K B T N O M Z Y
O C T O P U S B W F
R D C M F D B L P I
S S T A R F I S H S
E E L J N Z J W Q H
C P G N W H A L E J
W D O L P H I N W R
```

WORD LIST
CORAL REEF
DOLPHIN
EEL
JELLYFISH
OCTOPUS
SEAHORSE
STARFISH
WHALE

MAZE

Draw a line from start to finish.

START

FINISH

SEARCH

Look at the picture and write how many of each you can find.

gumdrops

basket

rabbits

ducks

colored eggs

jelly beans

244

DOT-TO-DOT

Connect the dots from 1-50.
Color the picture.

SOLVE THE CODE

Use the code to answer the question.

CODE

	1	2	3	4	5
(turtle)	P	R	C	U	L
(star)	B	R	U	M	X
(seahorse)	X	I	U	K	O
(fish)	T	V	N	K	P
(shell)	A	L	Z	Q	Y

What has two hands but can't clap?

1	3	2	5	3	4

___ ___ ___ ___ ___ ___

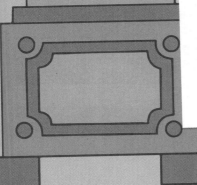

HIDDEN PICTURE

Find and circle the hidden pictures.

| lollipop | donut | rainbow | house | flower |

| car | notebook | gift | lightbulb | boat |

WORD SCRAMBLE

How many words can you make from the letters in **TRAIN STATION**?

1. _____

2. _____

3. _____

4. _____

5. _____

6. _____

7. _____

8. _____

9. _____

10. _____

11. _____

12. _____

13. _____

14. _____

15. _____

16. _____

17. _____

18. _____

19. _____

20. _____

21. _____

22. _____

10 = GOOD   15 = GREAT   20+ = BRILLIANT!

© School Zone Publishing 06339

WHAT DO YOU KNOW?

Read each sentence.
Circle **true** or **false**.

1. The green fish has spots.
   true   **false**

2. All of the fish are blue.
   true   **false**

3. The red fish is bigger than the green fish.
   true   **false**

4. There are 3 fish in the picture.
   true   **false**

5. All of the fish are swimming left to the worm.
   true   **false**

6. The orange fish has stripes.
   true   **false**

FOLLOW THE PATH

Help the kangaroo find his way home.
Start at **12** and count by **twos**.

Start

18	20	12	14	16	24	30	35	28	32
12	15	29	37	18	20	60	52	45	40
22	30	28	26	24	22	30	35	40	42
43	32	34	45	38	52	46	48	50	58
52	47	36	38	40	42	44	62	52	60
55	72	70	68	56	58	82	56	54	73
62	74	67	66	64	62	60	58	90	88
88	76	78	80	82	71	76	92	94	96
90	87	70	76	84	86	88	90	97	98
87	93	76	81	77	63	52	99	89	100

Finish

SEARCH

Look at the picture and write how many of each you can find.

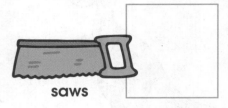

saws

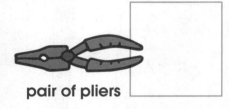

pair of pliers

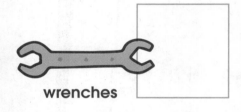

wrenches

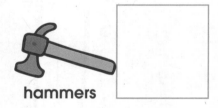

hammers

screwdrivers

screws

LEARN TO DRAW

Follow the steps to draw a dinosaur.
Color the picture.

STEP 1:

STEP 2:

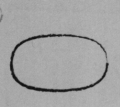

STEP 3:

STEP 4:

WHAT'S DIFFERENT?

Find and circle **6** things that are different in **picture A** and **picture B**.

Picture A

Picture B

HODGEPODGE

Each  has one that looks exactly like it.
Draw a line between each of the matching pairs.

SOLVE THE CODE

Use the code to answer the question.

CODE

	A	B	C	D	E
5	P	E	C	U	L
4	B	I	U	M	X
3	X	R	U	K	O
2	T	V	N	K	V
1	A	L	R	Q	Y

What can run but not walk?

$\overline{\text{1A}}$ $\overline{\text{3B}}$ $\overline{\text{4B}}$ $\overline{\text{2E}}$ $\overline{\text{5B}}$ $\overline{\text{3B}}$

258

SOLVE THE CODE

Follow the directions.
Then read the message that is left.

Color the **Y** boxes red.
Color the **C** boxes blue.
Color the **J** boxes orange.
Color the **H** boxes green.
Color the **Z** boxes purple.

Y	I	C	J	Z	L	I	K	E	C	J
R	E	D	C	J	Z	Y	H	J	Y	C
H	Z	Y	F	L	O	W	E	R	S	H
A	N	D	Y	P	U	R	P	L	E	Z
C	J	B	A	L	L	O	O	N	S	.

Write the hidden message.

_____

_____

WHAT DO YOU KNOW?

Read each sentence.
Circle **true** or **false**.

1. There are 4 birds in the picture.
   true   **false**

2. There is 1 red bird.
   true   **false**

3. There are 2 green birds.
   true   **false**

4. All of the birds are on the tree.
   true   **false**

5. The purple bird has a blue beak.
   true   **false**

6. The red bird has an orange beak.
   true   **false**

FOLLOW THE PATH

Help the turtle get to his friends at the pond.
Follow the path of odd numbers from **1** to **49**.

Start

1	3	14	6	90	4	42
66	5	7	9	11	13	30
64	32	12	22	54	15	18
27	25	23	21	19	17	24
29	34	10	16	82	98	48
31	33	35	37	14	50	6
68	80	78	39	58	88	98
72	10	2	41	62	20	26
42	84	94	43	45	47	49

Finish

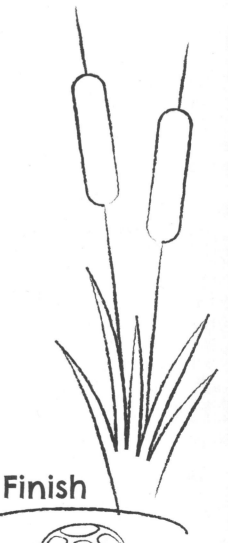

TIC-TAC-TOE

Find the words that go together.
Look across, down, and diagonally.

fish	key	five
bug	jump	four
star	blue	two

ball	rain	bat
lemon	butterfly	green
robin	down	red

sun	big	goat
wet	rain	two
star	old	snow

rose	ant	red
fox	bus	ten
blue	red	yellow

262

SEARCH & FIND

Look at the picture and write how many of each you can find.

rolling pin	plates	glasses	spoons

MAZE

Draw a line from start to finish.

START

FINISH

264

WHAT'S DIFFERENT?

Find and circle **6** things that are different in **picture A** and **picture B**.

Picture A

Picture B

COLORING

Color the picture.

- 🔴 = red
- 🔵 = blue
- 🟢 = green
- 🟡 = yellow
- 🟣 = purple
- 🩷 = pink

SOLVE THE CODE

Write the sums.
Use the code to solve the riddle.

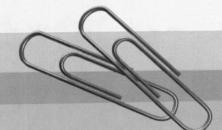

E	K	M
22 + 14	38 + 11	49 + 8

T	L	F
14 + 40	27 + 13	25 + 7

A	E	R
16 + 5	29 + 23	42 + 36

Where is the best place to buy bugs?

A ___ ___ ___ ___   ___ ___ ___ ___ ___ ___
   32 40 36 21   57 21 78 49 36 54

WHAT DO YOU KNOW?

Read each sentence.
Circle **true** or **false**.

Orange Frogs	🐸	🐸	🐸	🐸	🐸		
Green Frogs	🐸	🐸	🐸	🐸	🐸	🐸	
Blue Frogs	🐸	🐸	🐸	🐸	🐸	🐸	🐸
Yellow Frogs	🐸	🐸	🐸	🐸	🐸		

1. There are 6 green frogs.

   true   **false**

2. There is an equal number of orange and yellow frogs.

   true   **false**

3. 6 frogs are more than 7 frogs.

   true   **false**

4. There are more than 20 frogs altogether.

   true   **false**

5. There are less orange frogs than blue frogs.

   true   **false**

6. 4 frogs are fewer than 2 frogs.

   true   **false**

WHAT'S DIFFERENT?

Find and circle **6** things that are different in **picture A** and **picture B**.

Picture A

Picture B

SOLVE THE CODE

Use the clues to solve the problems.

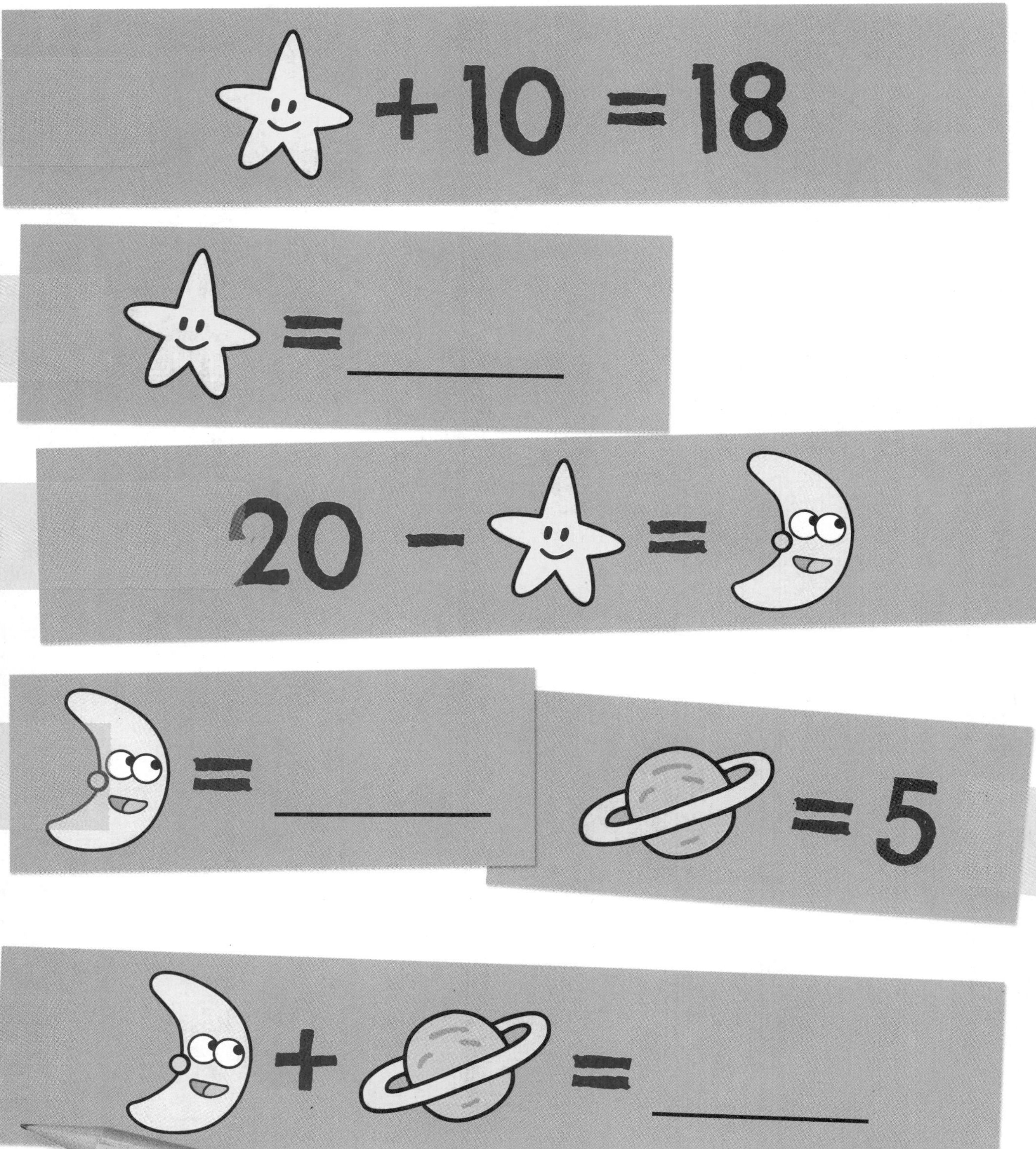

☆ + 10 = 18

☆ = _____

20 − ☆ = 🌙

🌙 = _____   🪐 = 5

🌙 + 🪐 = _____

MAZE

Draw a line from start to finish.

START

FINISH

Look at the picture on the left.
Color the graph for each one you find in the picture.

	1	2	3	4	5	6
(milk jar)						
SALE						
(cart)						
(bag)						

Use the graph above to solve the problems.

 + = _____   + (bag) = _____

 + (milk jar) = _____   + = _____

 + (milk jar) +  = _____

MATCHING PAIRS

Find and circle the picture that looks exactly like this one:

DOT-TO-DOT

Connect the dots from 1-50.
Color the picture.

© School Zone Publishing 06339

Find and circle the hidden pictures.

| starfish | shovel | lotion | apple | bone |

| sock | bucket | sandal | soda bottle | cap |

WORD SCRAMBLE

How many words can you make from the letters in **BEACH TOWEL** ?

1. _____
2. _____
3. _____
4. _____
5. _____
6. _____
7. _____
8. _____
9. _____
10. _____
11. _____

12. _____
13. _____
14. _____
15. _____
16. _____
17. _____
18. _____
19. _____
20. _____
21. _____
22. _____

10 = GOOD   15 = GREAT   20+ = BRILLIANT!

MAZE

Draw a line from start to finish.

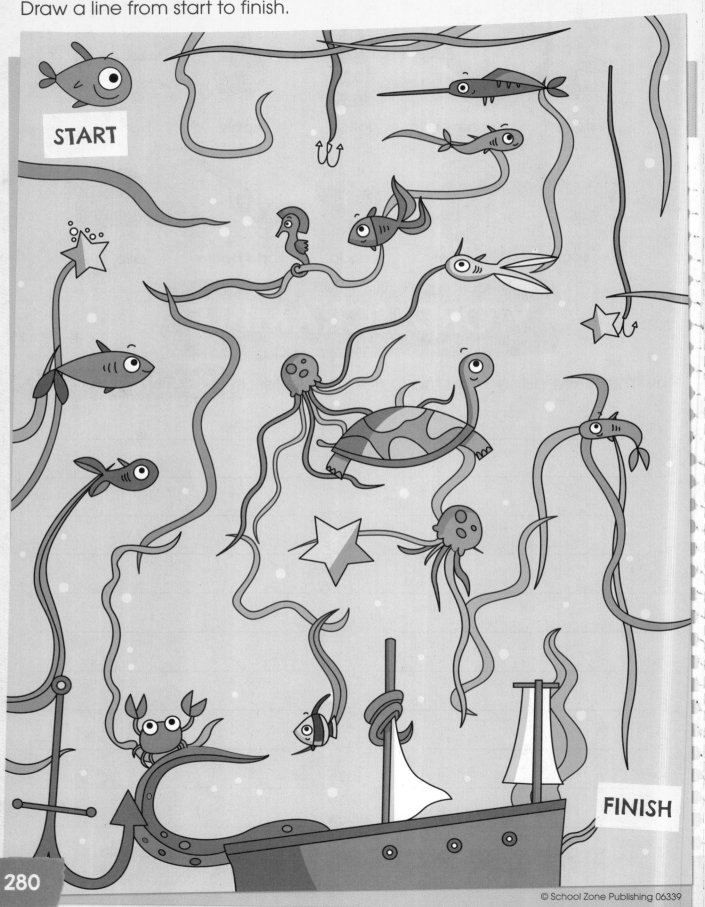

START

FINISH

WHAT'S DIFFERENT?

Find and circle **6** things that are different in **picture A** and **picture B**.

Picture A

Picture B

LEARN TO DRAW

Follow the steps to draw a panda.
Color the picture.

STEP 1: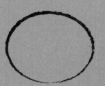

STEP 2:

STEP 3:

STEP 4:

STEP 5:

282

MISSING PUZZLE PIECES

Draw a line from each puzzle piece to its place in the puzzle.

MAZE

Draw a line from start to finish.

START

FINISH

SEARCH

Look at the picture and write how many of each you can find.

paintbrushes

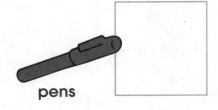

pens

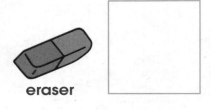

eraser

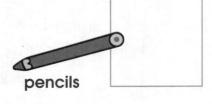

pencils

paper clips

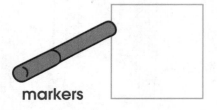

markers

286

MISSING PUZZLE PIECES

Draw a line from each puzzle piece
to its place in the puzzle.

DOT-TO-DOT

Connect the dots from 1-50.
Color the picture.

ORANGE
School Zone Publishing Company

HIDDEN PICTURE

Find and circle the hidden pictures.

fan

coffee mug

hat

crayon

pen

umbrella

tent

rubber
duck

light
bulb

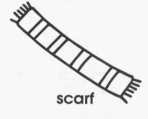
scarf

WORD SCRAMBLE

How many words can you make from the letters in **ON THE STAGE** ?

1. _____
2. _____
3. _____
4. _____
5. _____
6. _____
7. _____
8. _____
9. _____
10. _____
11. _____

12. _____
13. _____
14. _____
15. _____
16. _____
17. _____
18. _____
19. _____
20. _____
21. _____
22. _____

10 = GOOD   15 = GREAT   20+ = BRILLIANT!

COLORING

Color the picture.

- ● = red
- ● = blue
- ● = green
- ● = orange
- ● = purple
- ● = black

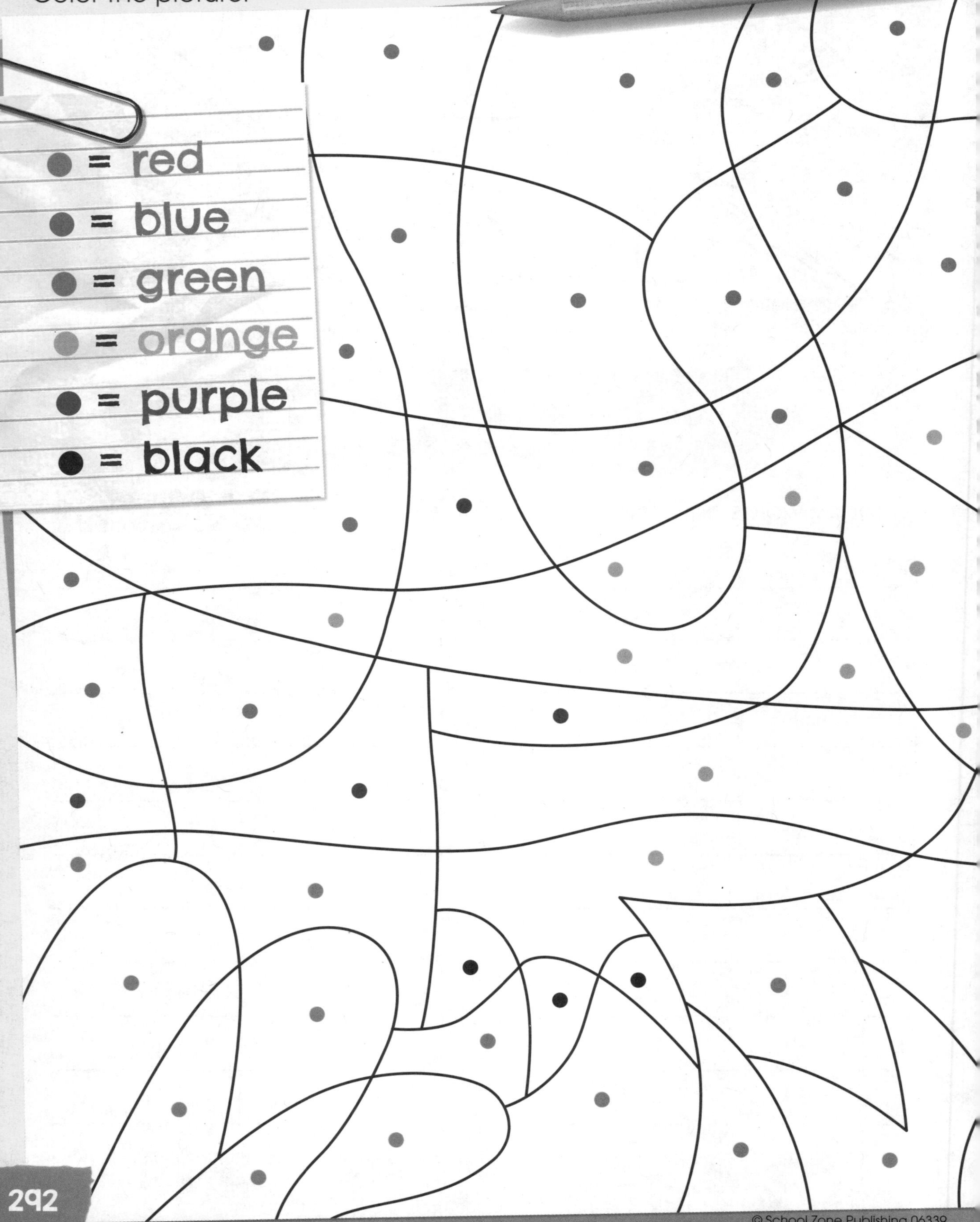

SEARCH

Look at the picture and write how many of each you can find.

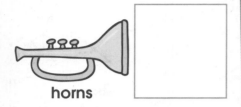
horns

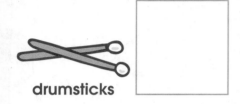
drumsticks

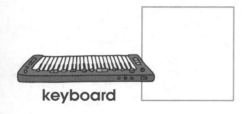
keyboard

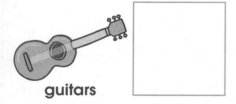
guitars

recorders

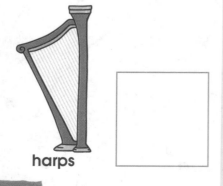
harps

294

© School Zone Publishing 06339

© School Zone Publishing 06339

ANSWER KEY

Page 1

Page 2

Page 3

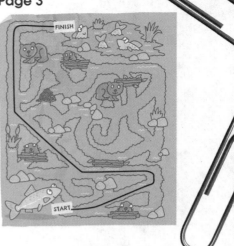

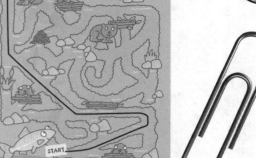

Page 4

Page 5

Some words are: or, it, at, to, do, art, aid, tap, tip, dip, air, tar, rod, oar, pot, pod, pad, rat, rip, dot, paid, part, pair, raid, toad, trap, tarp, roar, dart, drop, radio, ratio, patio, parrot, and raptor

Page 6

Page 7

Pages 8-9

Page 10

A BALD EAGLE

Page 11

```
F X R D F R I E N D
R M D A D P S N Z O
Z G R N K Q E T H L
Y Z S U J K Z L A D
T C I N Z I C P U Z
K M S C L T X M N B
Q K T L B A B O T B
T W E E I N M Z Z B
D B R O T H E R V G
B A B Y F Z B R N P
```

ANSWER KEY

Page 12

1. false
2. false
3. true
4. true
5. false
6. true

Page 13

Page 14

Pages 16-17

6 bones
4 butterflies
3 flowers
2 fish
9 rocks
11 trees

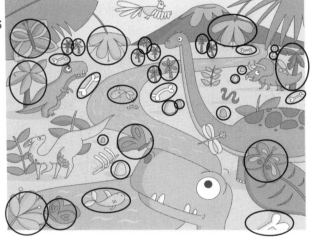

Page 18

K	H	O	W	Z	B	M	A	N	Y
Q	Z	M	O	N	T	H	S	K	B
A	R	E	Z	Q	B	K	I	N	Q
Q	B	A	K	Z	Y	E	A	R	?

Answer:
There are 12 months in a year.

Page 19

Finished drawing

Pages 20-21

Page 22

Page 23

```
L H E J L W U L S H
U W G V H Z J Q H C
Y N G H J Q H M O L
K P K R Z N O S E O
B L T I B A L L A W
D A C O R B Q K O N
H A T Z P D C H S L
I S B Y V U R I N G
F L O W E R P W J J
N G K C F U N B J W
N X V Z W P J E F Q
```

Page 24

GOLDFISH

Page 25

ANSWER KEY

Page 26

Page 27

Page 28

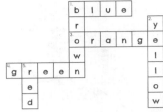

Pages 30-31

Page 32

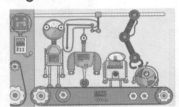

Page 33

A MAYFLY

Page 34

Page 35

Pages 36-37

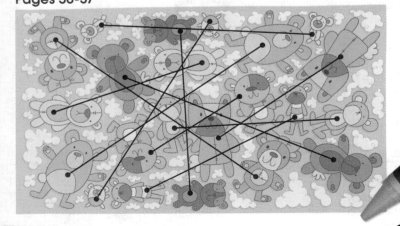

ANSWER KEY

Pages 38-39

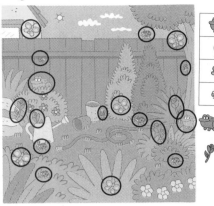

	1	2	3	4	5	6	7	8	9	10

🐸 + 🦋 = _7_   🐞 + 🦋 = _13_

🥕 + 🐜 = _12_   🐸 + 🥕 = _6_

🐸 + 🐞 + 🐸 = _12_

Page 40

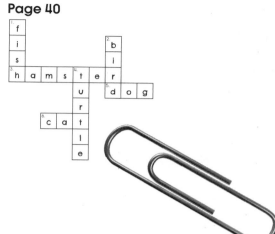

Page 41

Page 42

```
L G Y E L L O W D
B A M K Y H T H G
G N B L A C K I H
R C U R Z I N T E
E Q F B L U E E O
E I C S Q V J B P
N K P U R P L E L
R J X T D E M V W
B R O W N H R E D
```

Page 43

the starfish

Page 44

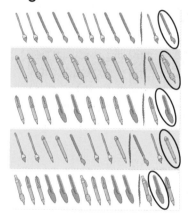

Page 45

Pages 46-47

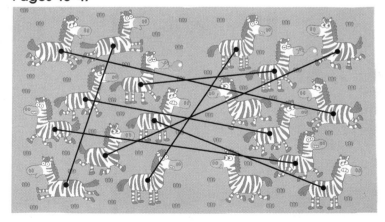

Page 48

Page 49

a snailer

Page 50

```
L X X W K D R Y I
P G X H H B H Y X C
G R A S S K P D M N
H B F Z F I R S S K S
C R E A M T E H K B
I S H A K E Y F S Y
C J I N Z J M J J X
E U W A L K O N Q S
A S U M M E R M Z U
L U N O G V F A F N
I C E C R E A M W G
```

Page 51

1. false
2. false
3. true
4. true
5. false
6. false

ANSWER KEY

Page 52

```
X S T B L T P N S P
T B E E O N K U H F
M Q O A M F G X M O
I O V R S T D U R X
X W C L B P G R Q B
R L Q R A B B I T H
B A T Z Z O D K L B
O H J G D U C K O N
U X T F G Z H B V V
D E E R C P B E Q F
```

Page 53

Page 54

Page 55

Some words are: in, am, an, pin, pig, pan, man, cap, can, gap, map, ping, main, pain, gain, camp, magic, and panic.

Page 57

Page 58

1. true
2. true
3. false
4. false
5. true
6. false

Page 59

a rain-deer

Page 60

Page 61

Page 64

Page 65

1. true
2. false
3. false
4. false
5. false

Pages 66-67

Page 68

ANSWER KEY

Page 69

```
P I C T U R E V U T M
I S F A E Q H L E D G
L C K B A T H T U B Z
L A T L J D B C L J E
O C J E P Y B O O K Q
W Z F B A V Z I F N G
K R S P I O V E N U S
I S O A P X N K G R I
Y W U O O B Q R M U N
L A M P R E A U X L K
V B P H M D S G O H N
```

Page 70

Page 71

```
¹b l o c k s
           ²b
       ³b o a t
       a      l
       l      e
⁴d o l l
d
r
u
m
```

Pages 72-73

Pages 74

Page 75

Finished drawing

Page 76

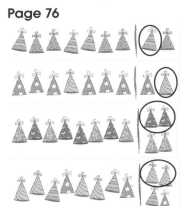

Page 78

Start

```
10  30  10  70  80  90
50  40  20  60  70  40
60  50  30  40  90  60
70  80  70  50  60  70
80  90  30  40  50  80
20  10  20  30  100 90
```

Finish

Page 79

```
        ¹m
        o
        u
  ²b a k e
        l
        o
        c
³s a c k
p
i
⁴n e s t
```

Page 80

Page 81

2 + 🐟 = 4

 🐟 = __2__

🐟 + 🐟 = 10

 🐟 = __8__

© School Zone Publishing 06339

301

ANSWER KEY

Pages 82-83

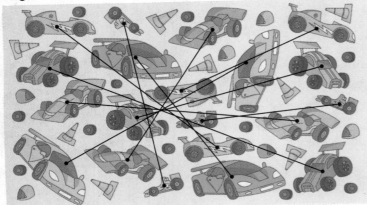

Page 84
trouble

Page 85

```
S W E A T E R  B  J  W
K  R A R P D Q U E  U
I  N  S Y V A C O A T  T
R  T  H  I  J  S H O E S  I  L  N  I
L  K  R C A K Y D P  H
W O  T  Z F  P U B  D  T
H  B G  I  E  A  E  H  R  S
F  X T  L  S  N  J  V  E  Q
L  N K G M T  T  J  A  S  I  C
G L O V E S  D  R  C
```

Page 86

Page 87

Page 88

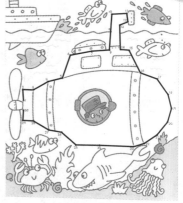

Page 89

Page 90

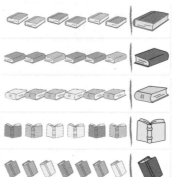

Page 91

302

ANSWER KEY

Pages 94-95

Page 96

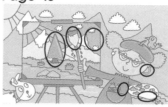

Page 97

```
R T M G R Y N B S
I K I T E J Z A Q
X R S B U D O L L
L C A R D S W L N
M Q L B F K A E P
A H R W Z H V C U
B L O C K S O A Z
Y P B M D B U T Z
C X O J B U D F L
G E T P K V I O E
```

Page 98

1. true
2. false
3. true
4. false
5. false
6. true

Page 99

Pages 100-101

4 snails
2 grasshoppers
1 bee
5 spiders
3 dragonflies
1 centipede

Pages 102-103

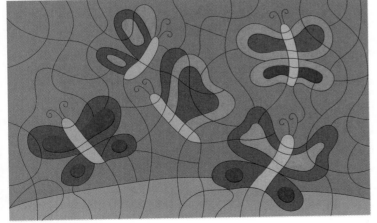

Page 104

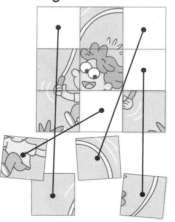

ANSWER KEY

Page 105

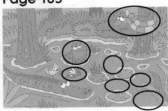

Page 106

ALL OF THEM

Page 107

J	Q	H	O	W	Z	M	A	N	Y
Z	X	I	N	C	H	E	S	Q	J
X	A	R	E	Z	X	I	N	J	X
Q	Z	A	J	Q	F	O	O	T	?

Answer:
There are 12
inches in a foot.

Page 108

T	E	B	Q	X	P	O	T	A	T	O	D
O	R	A	N	G	E	L	N	J	R	Z	Y
M	D	N	S	Y	A	P	R	I	C	O	T
A	C	A	L	O	R	W	E	M	A	I	S
T	Q	N	C	H	W	O	L	A	R	A	P
O	C	A	P	P	L	E	A	J	R	Z	M
V	P	T	K	D	B	B	F	C	O	R	N
C	H	E	R	R	Y	K	T	U	T	Z	I
U	N	B	E	R	A	F	H	V	O	Q	F
Y	T	I	P	U	M	P	K	I	N	Y	N
J	G	V	U	N	G	S	Z	G	M	H	K

Page 109

Page 110

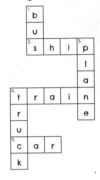

1. b
   u
2. s h i p
3. p
   l
   a
4. t r a i n
   r   e
   u
5. c a r
   k

Page 111

Page 112

5 snakes
3 frogs
1 woodpecker
4 turtles

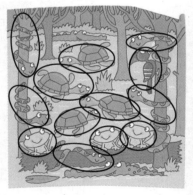

Page 114

Page 115

Pages 118-119

3 drums
1 toy car
5 toy boats
4 toy soliders
2 yo-yos
1 jack-in-the-box

Page 120

304

ANSWER KEY

Page 121

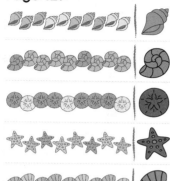

Page 122

a cosmonaut

Page 123

Page 124

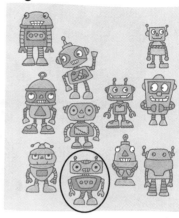

Page 125

 + 3 = 9

 = _6_

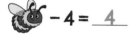 = 14

= _8_

− 4 = _4_

Pages 126-227

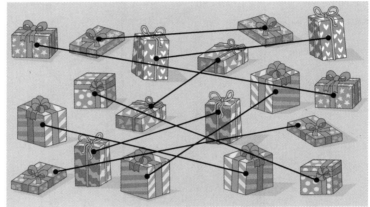

Page 128

Page 129

```
            w
            i
            n
        ²s u n n y
            o
    ³c       w
    l
  ⁴f o g g y
    u
    d
⁵r a i n y
```

Page 130

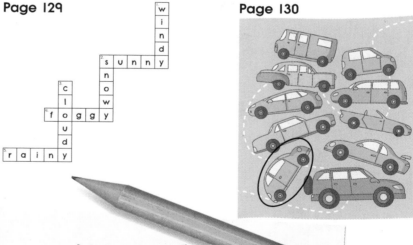

Page 131

ANSWER KEY

Pages 132-133

Pages 134-135

1 balloon
4 noisemakers
3 gifts
5 party hats
4 pieces of cake
2 candles

Page 136

Page 137

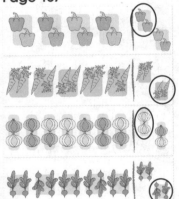

Page 138

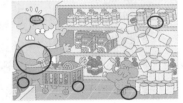

Page 139

A FINGERNAIL

Page 140

Page 141

1. false
2. true
3. false
4. true
5. true
6. false

Page 142

306

ANSWER KEY

Page 143

Pages 144-145

Page 146

Page 147

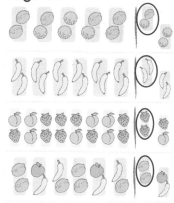

Page 149

3 rattlesnakes
2 toads
5 lizards
1 vulture

Pages 150-151

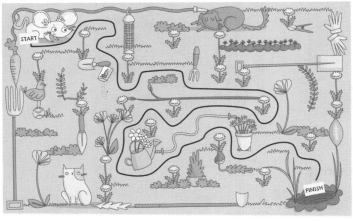

Page 152

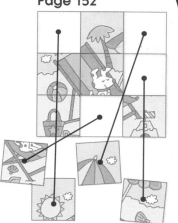

ANSWER KEY

Page 153

Page 154

Page 155

X	V	T	H	E	Y	P	G	O	V	P
V	P	X	K	V	P	X	V	P	K	X
P	X	A	R	O	U	N	D	V	X	P
K	V	K	X	V	V	K	X	P	V	K
I	N	P	S	C	H	O	O	L	S	.

Page 156

A BEDBUG

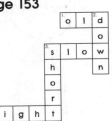

Page 157

Page 158

Page 159

Pages 160-161

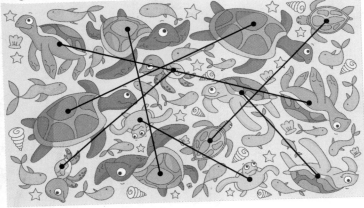

Page 162

Page 163

Some words are: say, sea, red, yes, sly, rye, sad, ear, day, dye, dry, lay, are, ray, easy, sale, read, rely, real, seal, area, ears, days, lady, dare, relay, salad, and already

Page 164

Page 165

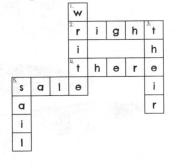

ANSWER KEY

Page 166

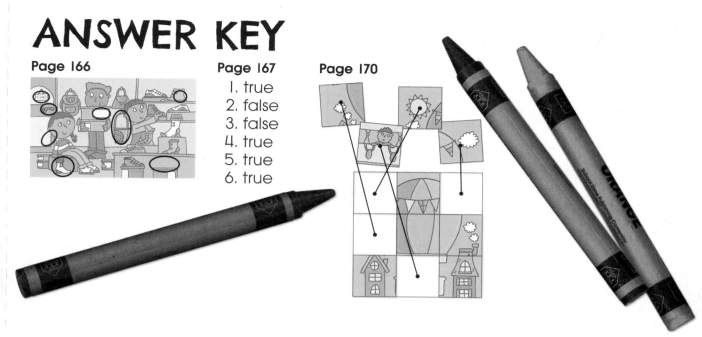

Page 167

1. true
2. false
3. false
4. true
5. true
6. true

Page 170

Page 171

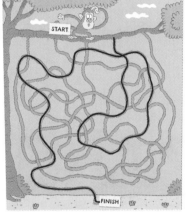

Page 172

Page 173

Pages 174-175

Page 176

Page 177

Some words are: am, an, us, me, at, as, tea, tan, ant, ate, ten, eat, sum, see, men, sea, sun, man, same, nuts, team, nets, nest, seen, stun, stem, tune, tuna, meet, east, menu, meat, mean, mast, mats, ants, aunt, tense, and steam

ANSWER KEY

Page 178

Page 179

A TURKEY

Page 180

```
C (T R A I N) Q L (B) H
P  R F R K S W M O P
A  U (G R) F F B N A G
(S  C O O T E R) O T A
Q  K X C R B E I V I
D  J D K J (C A R) Z R
I  S O E C L U L H P
G  A U (T A X I) V H L
G  D E Y Z I T D X A
E  N K C M T Y (V A N)
R  V (T A N K E R) W E
```

Page 181

1. false
2. true
3. false
4. false
5. true
6. true

Page 182

Page 183

Page 184

	1.				2.	
	o	r	a	n	g	e
					r	
3.	4.				a	
b	a	n	a	n	a	
	p				p	
	p			5.	p	
	l			p	e	a	r
					s	
6.						
l	e	m	o	n		

Page 185

Pages 186-187

Page 188

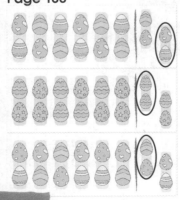

Page 189

Page 190

Page 191

SNEAKERS

Page 192

1. false
2. true
3. false
4. true
5. true
6. false

310

ANSWER KEY

Page 193

Pages 194-195

3 bananas
1 apricod
5 apples
2 pears
4 oranges
2 peaches

Pages 196-197

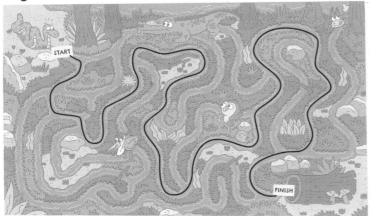

Page 198

Page 199

Page 200

a jitterbug

Page 201

```
J S H Q W P U M P K I N J E
W A F A W C W G H O S T W S
S F V H U W R F P L X G H N
P N A K C N W S W B A T J W
I M Y M O Q T W T X C M K L
D X D N T L P E W M X J V E
E S Y Z B R A V D W M W X B
R Z C G O G W N W H L E L O
W V P H L M Q D T Y O W S N
E N R C B W B P Q E O U N R
B W N B X K W I V W R W S P
G O B L I N V F E G H N L E
M O O N K M A S K W C A T I
```

Page 202

Pages 204-205

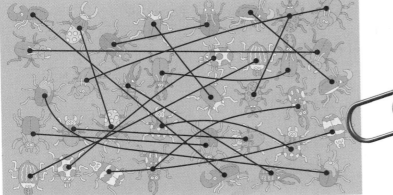

ANSWER KEY

Page 206

Page 207

1. true
2. false
3. false
4. true
5. true
6. false

Page 208

Page 209

Some words are: he, us, or, so, on, go, use, son, she, sun, hog, her, hug, ore, rug, our, run, shoe, hero, hour, nose, gone, sour, sore, sure, snug, house, heron, snore, horse, green, nurse, and hunger

Page 210

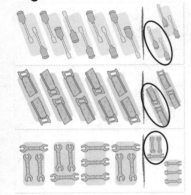

Page 211

Page 212

booberry pie and I scream

Page 213

```
T T A H I P P O K Q
I Q K J K R S A E M
G Z N O X R H I N O
E L E P H A N T L N
R L B J F Q Z D N K
H I V Q E B E A R E
M O X I B C B V J Y
I N X H P I R S F K
V Y M C E P A N D A
G I R A F F E L B M
```

Pages 216-217

4 crows
2 crescent moons
3 pumpkins
1 skeleton
5 black cats
1 witches hat

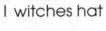

Page 218

Page 219

```
T U R T L E T J C O
F R O G F I S H C O
Q U E O L R P O N D
A B Z K J S W A M P
C R K P E O O K P S
H F X M Q V B Y C F
Z L I L Y P A D A I
I Y C A T T A I L O
G Y I N B X I T R D
B U O M O Z E B D O
```

312

ANSWER KEY

Pages 220-221

Page 222
1. false
2. true
3. false
4. false
5. true
6. false

Page 223

Pages 224-225

Pages 226-227

Page 228

Page 229
1. true
2. false
3. true
4. false
5. true
6. false

ANSWER KEY

Page 230

$\text{❄} + 3 = 12$

$\text{❄} = \underline{9}$

$\text{❄} + \text{❄} = 19$

$\text{❄} = \underline{10}$

$\text{❄} - \text{❄} = \underline{1}$

Page 231

People		
and	pat	red
dad	mom	brother
blue	the	sing

Animals		
did	eat	cat
bake	rabbit	do
dog	come	sit

Places		
sad	big	school
small	hot	zoo
happy	cold	beach

Things		
ball	talk	ju
run	blue	
wide	sheep	

Pages 232-233

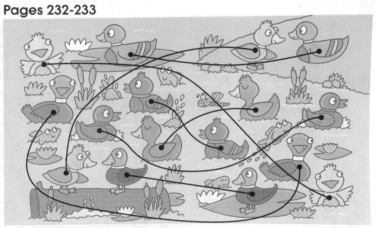

Page 234

Page 235

Some words are: we, me, am, bad, web, raw, are, war, ram, bed, mad, draw, warm, wear, rare, read, made, dear, bare, area, bear, beam, dare, brew, beard, bread, and dream

Page 236

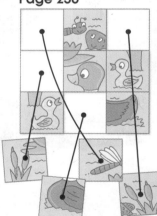

Page 237

ANSWER KEY

Pages 238-239

Page 240

Page 241

Pages 242-243

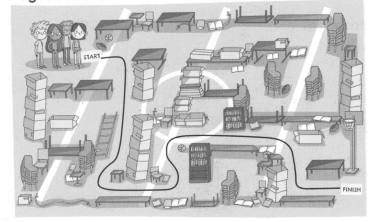

Pages 244-245

2 gumdrops
1 basket
5 rabbits
3 ducks
4 colored eggs
1 jelly beans

Page 246

Page 247
A CLOCK

ANSWER KEY

Page 248

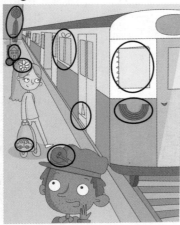

Page 249

Some words are: an, on, it, to, in, at, is, as, or, so, no, ton, inn, son, sit, art, sat, ran, air, ant, sir, rat, not, oat, tin, tan, oar, soar, tint, tart, iron, into, rain, stain, snort, roast, toast, and train

Page 250

1. true
2. false
3. false
4. false
5. true
6. true

Page 251

Pages 252-253

3 saws
1 pair of pliers
5 wrenches
4 hammers
2 screwdrivers
5 screws

Page 255

Pages 256-257

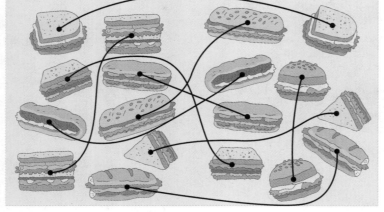

Page 258

A RIVER

Page 259

Y	I	C	J	Z	L	I	K	E	C	J
R	E	D	C	J	Z	Y	H	J	Y	C
H	Z	Y	F	L	O	W	E	R	S	H
A	N	D	Y	P	U	R	P	L	E	Z
C	J	B	A	L	L	O	O	N	S	.

316

ANSWER KEY

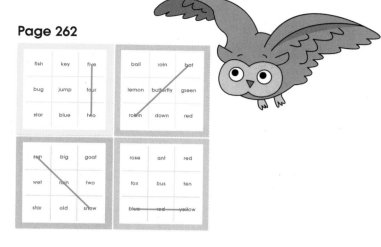

Page 260
1. false
2. true
3. false
4. true
5. false
6. true

Page 261

Start

	3	14	6	90	4	42
66	5	7	9	11	13	30
64	32	12	22	54	15	18
27	25	23	21	19	17	24
29	34	10	16	82	98	48
31	33	35	37	14	50	6
68	80	78	39	58	88	98
72	10	2	41	62	20	26
42	84	94	43	45	47	49

Finish

Page 262

Page 263

1 rolling pin
5 plates
4 glasses
3 spoons

Page 264

Pages 265

Pages 266-267

Page 268

A FLEA MARKET

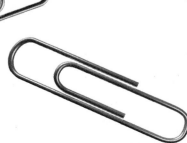

Page 269
1. true
2. true
3. false
4. true
5. true
6. false

Page 270

ANSWER KEY

Page 271

$$\text{⭐} + 10 = 18$$

$$\text{⭐} = \underline{8}$$

$$20 - \text{⭐} = \text{🌙}$$

$$\text{🌙} = \underline{12} \qquad \text{🪐} = 5$$

$$\text{🌙} + \text{🪐} = \underline{17}$$

Pages 272-273

Pages 274-275

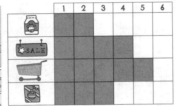

Page 276

Page 277

Page 278

Page 279

Some words are: to, he, be, oh, at, we, bee, act, ace, bet, who, tea, wet, toe, tow, two, web, bat, ate, how, cow, eat, hot, hat, eel, owl oat, cat, bow, lot, low, howl, heal, heat, hole, taco, bolt, chew, blow, boat, bath, each, echo, and whale

Page 280

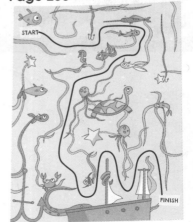

318

ANSWER KEY

Page 281

Page 283

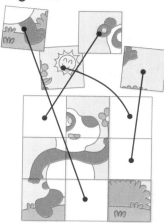

Pages 284-285

Pages 286-287

2 paintbrushes
4 pens
1 eraser
5 pencils
4 paper clips
3 markers

Page 288

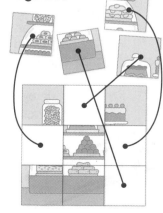

ANSWER KEY

Page 289

Page 290

Page 291

Some words are: oh, so, an go, as, he, to, no, at, ten, age, ton, the, eat, toe, ant, sea, see, set, hot, net, seat, teen, sent, than, tent, shoe, heat, goat, nest, nose, east, stone, ghost, taste, teeth, and toast

Pages 292-293

Pages 294-295

3 horns
5 drumsticks
1 keyboard
4 guitars
2 recorders
2 harps